Peter Eisenman

Peter Eisenman
Feints

edited by
Silvio Cassarà

SKIRA

Editor
Luca Molinari

Design
Marcello Francone

Editing
Marta Cattaneo
Francesca Ruggiero

Layout
Paola Ranzini

Translations
Leslie Ray for Language Consulting, Milan

The Italian edition of this book
was published on the occasions
of the exhibition
"Peter Eisenman. Contropiede",
Modena, Auditorium G. Monzani
18 June - 17 July 2005

First published in Italy in 2006 by
Skira Editore S.p.A.
Palazzo Casati Stampa
via Torino 61
20123 Milano
Italy
www.skira.net

Printed and bound in Italy. First edition

ISBN-13: 978-88-7624-378-3
ISBN-10: 88-7624-378-X

Distributed in North America by Rizzoli
International Publications, Inc., 300 Park
Avenue South, New York, NY 10010.
Distributed elsewhere in the world
by Thames and Hudson Ltd.,
181a High Holborn, London WC1V 7QX,
United Kingdom.

Contents

Subject-Object-Complement.
Brief Chronicle of an 'Unexpected' Architecture
Silvio Cassarà

Back in 1976, on the front cover of her book on *Five Architects*[1], Judith Turner published one of the most beautiful and significant images of the work of Peter Eisenman.

The photo, which is difficult to refer back to a specific "construction", especially when compared with what is shown in the text, rich in the most orthodox and canonical details of architecture—railings, panels, façades—shows the detail of an interior of House VI.

I believe this image still remains one of those that best summarise both the uniqueness of the work of Peter Eisenman and of the changes of a whole historical period that this could very well be selected to sum up.

The detail is noteworthy on account of the multiple interpretations, but above all because it is a kind of x-ray, the "blocked" image of a constantly changing system of thought, the word of a changing phrase, thought of and constructed, defined and indefinite, in expectation of its natural transcending, which is precisely what the work of Peter Eisenman is: a kind of fragment where it is possible to perceive—as the photographer has done—the system of overlaps between real and ideal that distinguishes it, where the system of use of colour and the presence of a structure of which the semantic reversal is perceivable—precisely in the difficulty of its individualization—, as is the alteration of the sense of function in the colouring of a staircase anchored to the ceiling opening up a tear on the ideal volume that implies it that is much more vast than that expressed in the third dimension.

And is the sensation that the photo gives not only abstraction, or at least not in the sense underlined by Tafuri[2]. It is the testimony of a way of conceiving design projects as an intellectual operation that goes beyond itself and manipulates the system of space: a space understood *à la* Baudrillard, as culture in fact[3].

Compared with what was happening or had happened in those years in the United States—the text and work of Venturi, the artistic expansionism of Meier, the activity of Gehry—Eisenman's design cycle was characterised by a link between design work and project culture that was unknown even to the work of Rem Koolhas, who was then more preoccupied with an analysis of urban systems than with their actual methodological application on the delimited scheme.

Eisenman was—as indeed he is—the American culture of intellectualised design work: a culture capable of facing the analysis of the entire linguistic apparatus on the basis of a double knowledge, the European and the local; which others limited to the body of modernist "Memory", whether purified or not of the heroic system that had been its main European support.

House VI. Stairs

9

In his Foucault-style "desire to know", Eisenman was seeking destabilisation, heresy and transposition on the construction in a positivist vein of this total philosophical system capable of linking American pragmatism with European "idealities", in all the ways, on the various scales and with all the possible systems of diffusion.

Through the IAUS and with his magazine "Oppositions", "Skyline" or any sort of writing and lecture, relating himself to those new Italian tendencies on which Tafuri himself, showing no tenderness in his consideration of him, as indeed of any his contemporaries, was rather sceptical.

But his CV was more complexly structured. He could take advantage of an operational approach unknown to Europeans, an analytical apparatus of Italian culture that was absolutely unique, as were his frequentings of the world of the American conceptuality of Lewitt, Morris and Judd and of the merciless analyses that Rowe conducted of the systems of Corbu and Palladio, as well as of the thought on "philosophy" of Deleuze and Derrida (even if this was to occur in a later phase). That Deleuze whose formidable reading of Bacon provides sure support in the reading of the no longer cubist images of this architecture, such as that referred to above.

An architecture that absorbs a scientific curiosity for the conceptual absolute to be represented in the construction, ideally, above all, rather than formally.

House IV

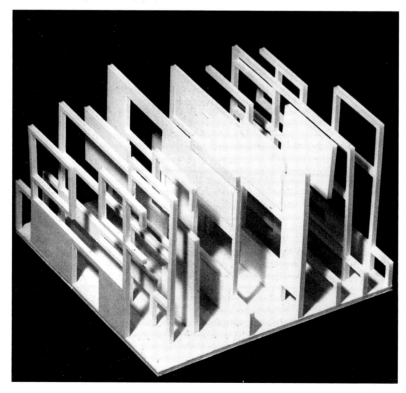

What the photo shows is that loss of bearings that Eisenman intends to portray as indeed he does portray it in the afunctional spaces where the principle of the overlapping of planes of cubist origin is dissolved in favour of the principle of coinciding formally and structurally indefinite planes. It is a rebellion against the principle of the norm that has no precedents if not in mannerist age, but that also scrutinises the intrinsic alluded to in the works of Bramante and Peruzzi.

It is the norm as a synthesis of the system of rules that, on the basis of the (now changed) relationship between man, nature and divinity, had expressed ethical principles and represented formal syntheses, that was the antagonist and was to be investigated so as "to be" the antagonist to reconstitute a personal essentiality and an ideal autonomy.

A formidable ideological platform was therefore perfected with his doctorate thesis, intended to unhinge the unproductive tranquillity of a linguistic system arising on the basis of the readings of Colin Rowe, Tafuri and Chomsky to overturn the approach to planning, making it the representation of his genetic process, which his early production expresses perfectly.

The cycle of houses begun with the studies on *frontality vs rotation*, which had also been experimented with and immediately abandoned by Meier, moved on after the initial projects to specify the research objectives and allow the "deep structure" of the architecture to emerge, assimilating De Stjil to arrive at a non-definitive system of architecture to reflect the torment of the analysis of matrices flowing into forms that nevertheless did not communicate certainties.

House IV

This architecture was supposed to arrive at – or rather to reveal – its own self-estrangement and flow into a limbo of autonomy realised through the use of elements of neutrality, whose rigour was to destroy the sense of the context in order to reconstitute it; and to place itself beyond typology, beyond function, to form an archetype. Every sign can be structure and every structure can have a multiplicity of readings, embodying an absolute universality. Not formal, or at least not necessarily formal.

The sketches for House II are explicit.

We are well beyond the abstractive force spoken of by Tafuri. Discussing House VI, William Gass speaks, not coincidentally, of a Copernican world[4].

No other contemporary architect has put together such an ideological apparatus from which to draw and to update, linking their product to the expression of its essence. Because the purpose of this work is not that of theoretical speculation, but of its practical realisation.

"The work resides in a pre-existing universe, separated not in a temporal but an absolute sense"[5].

The endless sequence of designs of his doctorate study, where the whole body of the Modern Movement is dealt with, building by building, underlines both the finalities and the value of the "method". If analysing History, especially recent History, was a generational fact that was common in those years, there were few who transcended the system of investigation to formulate a kind of treatise to be constantly verified, irrespective of the 'blackmail' of the verification of the construction.

Eisenman appropriates and makes his own a role traditionally relegated to the critics or, in short, to the historians: those of the English school, the Rowes, the Framptons, and those of Italian origin, such as Tafuri and Rossi, the latter in many ways in a condition analogous to his own, that of an architect with a strong theoretical base, whatever it was and with the due—more than a few—differences.

Eisenman therefore lives and embodies this anything but comfortable position symbiotically.

It is not the critical awareness of a re-evoked age, *à la* Hejduk: it is the expression of an inexorable existential condition, whose work is ruinous for the constitution of an objective credibility of project work.

The seventies had been crucial for this verification process.

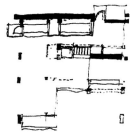

While the Five's natural distancing of themselves, taking up autonomous positions, led almost all to work in specific spheres in the shadow of the post-Lecorbusian matrix, Eisenman broadened the "centre" of his research.

It is the space that is investigated: the purpose is the perfecting of a system of meanings to be related together without symbolic finalities. The form will follow or result, or perhaps will not follow at all. But it will be complex.

This alters the relationships with History, which is the parameter of current reading of this generation.

That History whose "complex" renders sterile the Italian planning projected to analyse the city rather than architecture, loaded with presumed heroic values and "nostalgia" for a condition that reveals its own impotence, frozen in the dimension of memory and its fragments.

That History that provides Stirling with unpredictable and often disquieting compositional instruments, as is shown in that ideal city plan realised for monuments or, if you prefer, fragments of monumentality.

That History whose fragments Graves composed literally and of which Eisenman decomposed the materiality through the geometry of overlapping and coinciding analytical readings, assailing the bases of Vitruvian theory. The structural virtualism underlines, as Moneo notes[6], that Vitruvius did not mean that buildings had to be structural, but that they had to appear "structural".

In 1976, when House VI was completed, the Smith House (1967) and the Vanna Venturi House (1964) had already made their appearance, and the Gehry House and the definitive realisation of the British Art Center in Yale would soon see the light of day.

It would not be long till the evocative appearance of the World Theatre on the laguna, surely the most powerful and evocative, but also syncretic, realisation by Rossi. The theatre as universal metaphor.

House II

The main tendencies under way in Europe and in the USA were therefore defined in those years; they were already celebrated in one of the best biennial exhibitions ever to take place, with the homonymous title: the cohesiveness of the forms of Meier, with their intrinsic mnemonic value, the assemblage of "banal" and epidermal forms of Venturi, the unhinging of every grid by Gehry, the silent metaphysical poetry of Hejduk, that of the cubes and the *nine square grid*—so frequently taught *à la* Cooper—confirming the Transatlantic attention to a scale that allows a merciless control of the residential object and the uneasiness of Eisenman's cardboard houses in relation to the acquiescence to all manner of clientele.

If the Smith House was the ideal construction or ideality realised through the combined force of reason rendered abstraction in the power of every detail, House II finds its own force in rendering explicit difficulty in expressing totally the quantity of meanings included in its own condition of being prevalently structure. The house does not placate and does not intend to placate any form of conflict that is not conceptual. Rather, it records them.

While the diagrams of Richard Meier literally confirm the clarity of an ideal and real procedure – the routes, the structure, the light and anything else –, Eisenman's grids do not tend to define, if not in transformation, a process that excludes the function from the design course proper.

The interiority of this architecture is linked to an "absence" that does not have a geometric derivation. Having no functional finalities, aesthetics, shell, the site addresses an architecture understood as the manifestation of a void that has its own completeness and its own immanence.

As he himself was to write on the subject of the project for the Church of the 2000[7], "it is not a question of denying the function and the meaning of the object, but rather of discussing the legitimacy of the formal decision made in its name"; these statements underline the difficulty of comparative analyses on the specific, precisely on account of their ideal formulation, but they do help us understand the attitude towards a project work that is "other" than "cut off", as Rosalind Krauss writes on the modes of legitimisation of objects to preserve them[8].

The process of delegitimisation destroys hierarchical scales and works through decompositions and totalising partialities.

If Smith House tends towards unitariness, House II and the other houses tend towards fragmentation, which has now become the protagonist, as inferred from the assumptions of the theoretical studies on Terragni. Transformations, decompositions, criticism. Citing the text on the Italian architect – a text constantly updated over many years before its definitive recent publication – this is de facto the path legible and adopted by Eisenman, at least until now.

Far removed from Ville Savoye and from the Garches, whose frontality was considered excessive at a time when frontality vs rotation was adopted by the whole New York milieu.

And it was very present both in the works of Richard Meier, at least in the beginning, and in those of our protagonist.

But Terragni is more complex. Not all: fundamentally, but not only, that of the Casa del Fascio.

But it is also the most "analogous" in providing and placing itself as methodological exemplarity in the perfecting of the critical text, the rendering explicit of the reading of which is analysis and project together.

The amount of data—from the perspective of studies conducted—is staggering.

The building is taken as a critical text to be read in the cross-fade of analyses that place sequence, hierarchy, unity in crisis in favour of a reading that allows the fragmentation, the alternation, the oscillation, the disjunction of an apparently compact work to emerge.

A method that had in fact been adopted in relation to Palladio, in whom Rowe was interested, arriving at results that were divergent, or rather, easily directable towards formally tangible results.

This "History" confirms its own continuity—from Palladio to Terragni —and legitimises, or rather enunciates, the theoretical basis of its own operation.

It renders visible the "hidden" analytical and diagrammatic apparatus of architecture, that "inner structure" that is astructural and around which it is possible to play, interpolating the roles-object-subject, of which the "planned"—not the construction, note—is the primary goal.

The analytical basis of architecture can be revealed within what Tafuri was to define[9] as "disenchantment for those who recognise the desert as their own house" and whose complexities are at the moment relegated to the small-scale, at least to dimensions allowing an absolute control over the biographical process of formation of the project, with this procedure being itself a project.

The inevitable leap of scale too is almost generational.

Meier was to find himself facing the Getty problem, investigating the culture of fragmentation redeemed by architecture; Gehry was to affirm the urban value of the multiplicity of languages used inside the same project in an LA vein, from the Faculty of Law to Turtle Creek, the OMAs were to participate in the Competition for the Municipal Hall of The Hague on a scale that suited them, as well as reaffirming the success of the architecture of "Arbitrariness", wishing to use a definition that was nevertheless partial, in the preparation of the Exhibition on Deconstructivist architecture at the MOMA.

It is the Fin D'ouThou's house that, in 1985, Architectural Design[10] chose to represent one of the many reviews that American architecture undergoes on a cyclical basis.

In the issue in question there was the big business of Pelli's World Financial Center, the Arcadia of Graves' Winery, Meier's Frankfurt Museum, but also Columbus' project for the Osu Center.

The house, modest in dimensions, proposes the cross-reading of plan and elevations already studied in other projects and celebrated by House X. Small elegant interplays of Ls, capable of showing the expressive potentialities of the system of grids and assigning a degree of refined autonomy to every "situation", showing a maturity of control naturally and not forcedly intellectualised.

We are outside the "project", against the "project", in order to realise "another authentic project" and reappropriate it through the fragmentation of a general almost charismatic compactness.

The value of the principle of virtuality applied to architecture dissolves depth, sequence, function and hierarchy, but reconstitutes them, conserving a freshness in the "intrinsic criticality" that the rigour of the (ever-) present "ratio" of the grids relates back to architecture.

The archisculpture is complete.

It is not a place of denied memory: it is a place of reconstituted memory that, through the multiplicity of presences, allows a kind of perceptive individuality that seems to recall the magnificent introductory title to a book by John Hejduk, *In my father's room there are many mansions*. The "eyes that no longer see Le Corbusier" are replaced by those that see beyond. If on the threshold of the eighties, the presence of Eisenman's Architecture on the international panorama was a culturally consolidated fact, now it is also professionally palpable.

The predictable self-extinction of the Posts was to leave space from now on to a sector of research that was greatly broadened to embrace "expressionist" design currents: accumulable only as antithetical—if the term is correct—to an approach configurable within the linguistic canonicity.

Both Gehry and the paintings of Zaha Hadid fit within an a-historical tendency that does not have relations of a "mnemonic" type with architecture. And deeply pragmatic, at least for Gehry.

In common, if anything, there is the transcending of the typological system, in the shadow of which whole generations have been raised.

The great void that Eisenman intends to fill has to do with the stratification of existing and non-visible "texts" that affirm the atemporality of memory in the symbiosis between future, present and past.

This is what Deleuze treats as an example in the analytical reading of Proustian *Recherche*, affirming a concept confirmed also on the subject of a text by Bergson entitled "Matter and Memory".

House II

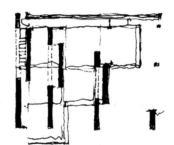
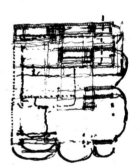
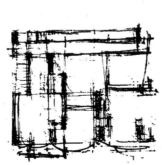
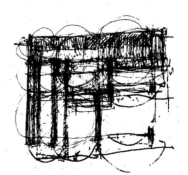

Arriving in this way at the concept of virtuality in architecture, which Eisenman himself was to specify in many speeches, where it is affirmed[11] that the virtual as reality in architectural space is a very different thing from the virtual in a broad and general sense.

"The Virtual in architecture is that part of the present that contains a memory of the past. The virtual in architecture has to do with Memory that exists in the innerness of architecture projected into the present".

Which is then the statement made by Deleuze and rendered operational on the subject of the statement whereby structural criticism has the object of determining the virtualities that pre-exist in the language, the work being itself structural when it proposes to express its own virtuality[12].

There emerge both the complexities and the pleasure in the intrinsic difficulty of making architecture by manoeuvring its real and virtual spaces in an unexpected manner.

This x-ray of the intrinsic systems explains the uniqueness of the method in the absence of a formal repertoire and in the presence of an immanent ideal system. The decanting of this architecture into the extended dimension is at this point inevitable and consequential: Already in '78 Cannaregio was the proof of this.

Or rather, the first confrontation with the context, amply historicised, incidentally, such as that of the district where Le Corbusier was supposed to intervene with his hospital.

A context that Eisenman denies and reconstitutes as a project negation in the large void with submerged historical schemes, bringing out the Tafurian "essential non-essentiality" in an atemporal dimension icily distant from the interventions of Rossi.

The cycle of houses is successfully concluded pouring a few manipulated images of the last House, XI, into the adventure of the reworking of the context. This is totally assimilated in the process of absolute invention of the space.

Cannaregio is a genuine moment of growth in the ideal system of this research, with its programme in a constant process of self-definition and of his way of placing himself in relation to a reality or a "future" professional reality, also much more restrictive than the area of Cannaregio.

Such as the project for the IBA in Berlin, where the simultaneous reading of the schemes of the site shuts the building up in a vice of grids that confirm the estrangement of nostalgia from the strategic system of confrontation with the past. And where the texture allows the many structures present in the building to emerge, entrusting unusual epidermal values to the colour.

If some projects can allow the emergence of a more literal and provocative decompositional approach, such as for the Aronoff Center or the Nunotami Headquarters in Tokyo, others, in parallel to the increasing professional commitment, confirm the trust in the system of diagrams as the only arm of ideal definition for every project, an arm, incidentally, enriched by the use of the computer, by now inseparable from it.

As for the scale, this has now become relatively indifferent, because still a tactical instrument of intervention.

The Guardiola House, one of the few houses that take their name from the owner, is exemplary in this regard, as Cannaregio had been a decade earlier, and as Romeo and Juliet were soon to be. But while the Guardiola is measured only in relation to itself, in a formidable experiment of control of the virtual, but also of affirmation of equilibrium between formal systems made architecture, Romeo and Juliet were to reintroduce an exterior, an outside, against which to be measured through the obviously known procedures.

Those that nobody like the author clarifies, as is his custom, and that it is nevertheless useless to subdivide temporally into one cycle or into a subsequent one. Those of the houses had exhausted the investigation on the discipline, but its contribution is the basis of comparison with the diagrams of outside. Those of the scheme of the fluid volumes of the Greater Columbus Convention Center, the constructed orography of the memorial in Berlin, or the problem of total planning of the Galizia City of Culture, managed with great boldness despite the functional complexity and an "other" out-of-scality where the relationship with the territory is more defined than ever.

And where the leap in scale has not compromised this timeless city of history, which repudiates any formal reference, citation, and obstinately reaffirms its own disciplinary mechanisms. Eisenman looks at this architecture, which looks within itself, in this exchange of unexpected roles. His is an inimitable career path: it is the universality of the individual in a world levelled out by intrusive information technology and made banal by pseudo-historicising formalism. Proud of having eliminated any wreckage of comforting mnemonic formalism traceable in any work of any great current protagonist from the process that leads to architecture, running the risk of self-eliminating for the sake of affirming the signic reduction of a language sometimes too cultured to be current.

But Peter Eisenman will continue to run this risk, looking at the architecture that looks inside itself from another point of view, almost like Cosimo di Rondò in "The Baron in the Trees", capable of looking at life and things from high up in a forest canopy, from where, like Peter, he does not intend to come down, because that is the dimension from which, in fact, to look at life and things. And at architecture.

[1] Judith Turner, *Judith Turner Photographs Five Architects*, Rizzoli, New York, 1980.

[2] M. Tafuri, *La sfera e il labirinto*, Einaudi, Turin, 1980, p. 360.

[3] J. Baudrillard, *America*, SE.

[4] William Gass, 'House VI', in *Progressive Architecture*, June 1977, p. 60.

[5] A+U 80:01, *Special Peter Eisenman*.

[6] R. Moneo, *Inquietudine teorica e strategia progettuale nell'opera di otto architetti contemporanei*, Electa, Architetti e Architetture.

[7] B. Zones, *Eisenmanarchitects 1988-98*.

[8] Rosalind Krauss, *Blurred Zones*.

[9] M. Tafuri, 'Giuseppe Terragni: Subject and Mask', in *Oppositions*, n. 11; *Lotus* n. 20.

[10] Architectural Design 55/12/85, Cross Currents of American Architecture.

[11] "Written into the Void", from an article originally written in 1997 and updated for the exhibition at the Mak.

[12] G. Deleuze, *Lo strutturalismo*, SE, p. 49.

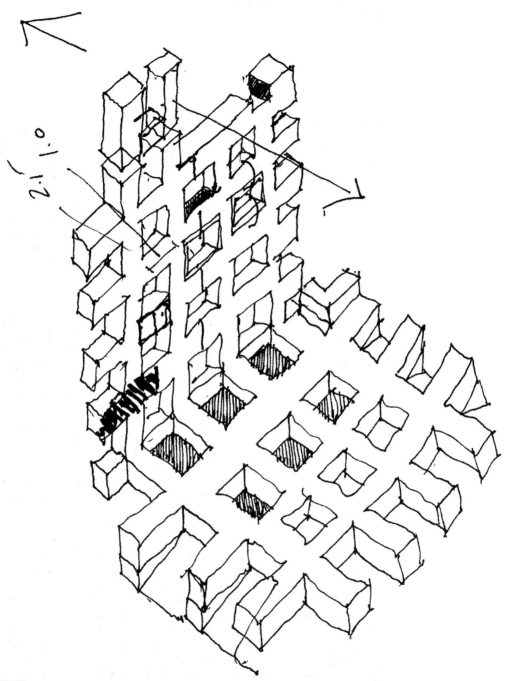

Diagram

What is a Diagram anyway?
Anthony Vidler

What, then, is a diagram?
Well, the dictionary definition allows a pretty wide sweep of possibilities. The Oxford English Dictionary traces the word from the Old French, "diagramme", out of the Greek "diagramma", from "dia", ("through", "across"), or and "graphein", something written, like a letter of the alphabet. Which takes diagram from simply something "marked out by lines", all the way through a geometrical figure, to a written list, a register, a gamut or scale in music. More precisely, and along the lines of its geometry, a diagram might be "a figure composed by lines", an "illustrative figure", a "set of lines, marks, or tracings". But it is the function of these traces that is important: a diagram serves something else. It illustrates a definition, aids in the proof of a proposition, it represents the course or results of any action or process.

How might it do this?
First, it doesn't, like a picture, represent the "exact appearance of an object". Rather it represents "symbolically". In this sense, it is an abstraction of what it represents, giving only "an outline or general scheme of it"; it exhibits "the shape and relations of its various parts" without imitating them. Through this abstraction it is able to signify variations, actions, or even mental processes. It is at once precise—giving form to a definition or statement—and vague—an outline or "general scheme"[1].

You used the word "symbolically." Is the diagram then a symbol?
Perhaps the most penetrating examination of the nature and role of diagrams was undertaken by Charles Sanders Peirce (1839-1914), in the context of his general theory of signs, his semiology. For Peirce, all thinking took place with signs, things which served "to convey knowledge of some other thing". which they were "said to *stand for*, or *represent*". A sign therefore always has an *object*, and the sign in turn excites an idea in the mind, a mental sign of the same object, or that which interprets the sign[2]. But, of course, all signs are not the same. Peirce distinguished three kinds of sign: the *Icon*, the *Index*, and the *Symbol*. The Icon is that kind of sign that is most like its object—"a sign which stands for its object because as a thing perceived it excites an idea naturally allied to the idea that object would excite"[3]. Most icons indeed are likenesses. In this definition, a photograph, or even a fragment of audio mimicry would be an icon. An Index, by contrast, holds no resemblance to its object, it simply points to it: "An *index* stands for its object by virtue of a real connection with it, or because it forces the mind to attend to that object"[4]. Peirce cites the barometer, that indicates the temperature, the weathervane that indicates the direction of the wind, or the pole star, from which we derive our sense of direction in na-

ture. And finally, the Symbol, which unlike the Icon or the Index, which are "non-declarative" signs, "is a sign naturally fit to declare that the set of objects, which is denoted by whatever set of indices may be in certain ways attached to it, is represented by an icon associated with it"[5].

But, given we accept this division, where does the diagram fit into this schema?

For Peirce, the diagram is neither Index nor Symbol, but rather a special kind of Icon. Here he distinguishes between three kinds of Icons: those that are more properly called images, or "hypoicons," that, as in the case of paintings, resemble their objects in many particulars; those that represent the character of their objects through parallelism, which he calls "images"; and those that mark out the internal and external relations of their objects in a more abstract way, analogously, that he calls "diagrams"[6].

What is the importance of the diagram to Peirce?

As a philosopher inquiring into the nature of thought through the use of signs, Peirce is naturally primarily interested in the diagram. It is, he believes, a *useful* sign for thinking: "A diagram is a kind of icon particularly useful", he writes, "because it suppresses a quantity of details, and so allows the mind more easily to think of the important features"[7]. This said, a diagram is most useful of all for the work of mathematics: "mathematical reasoning is diagrammatic", he repeats, as he investigates the thought processes of algebra and geometry, both of which employ diagrams as an integral part of their functioning[8]. More generally, he claims, all reasoning, whatever the object, is diagrammatic in form, as it works through abstraction to develop hypotheses and test them: "we construct an icon of our hypothetical state of things and proceed to observe it... We not only have to select the features of the diagram which it will be pertinent to pay attention to, but it is also of great importance to return again and again to certain features... But the greatest point of art consists in the introduction of certain *abstractions*"[9].

But doesn't this make the diagram simply a static and fixed version of one moment in thought, thus blocking any development?

No, because it is precisely through abstraction that allows the diagram to be, so to speak, productive, so that through permutation and transformation, the "characters of one diagram may appear in another"[10]. In this sense the diagram is both the instrument of thought and its mirror.

If that is the case, what about thought that is prospective, projective, and prognostic?

This is where the diagram truly comes into its own. Peirce gives examples of thought processes that, using diagrams, are transformed into "resolutions", or "determinations": a "plan" is a diagram, which is no more than a program for future action, based on the ideas and principles embodied in it. For Peirce, then, the diagram is, finally, a mental formula, a schematic device, by means of which we move from one thought to another. It is, by reason of its "general" nature, its abstraction, a vehicle for the production of new, and developing diagrams[11].

Does this not lead to what we might call a "fetishization" of the diagram?

Certainly not for Peirce: as an icon, or "schematic image," that embodies the meaning of its object—in the case of thought, a "general predicate"—it serves in itself only as an object, the observation of which produces another general predicate. In other words "the diagram itself is not what reasoning is concerned with", but rather it operates as a vehicle of transmission and production of reasoning[12].

Can you give a specific example?

In his essay on the philosopher-astronomer Johannes Kepler, whose work on the rotation of the planets after Tycho Brahe proved their elliptical orbits, Peirce found the key to Kepler's success in his method of reasoning, and this through the use of diagrams:

"His admirable method of thinking consisted in forming in his mind a diagrammatic or outline representation of the entangled state of things before him, omitting all that was accidental, observing suggestive relations between the parts of his diagram, performing divers experiments upon it, or upon the natural objects, and noting the results".

Here, Peirce admits that something more than the mathematical structures of reason had to come into play; something that characterized "high reasoning power". This he called "imagination". But this was not imagination in general—that "ocean-broad term, almost meaningless, so many and so diverse are its species"—nor was it the poetic imagination that conjures up the unknown. Rather, what Peirce saw in Kepler was a kind of "devil's imagination". Where, the "poet-imagination riots in ornaments and accessories" Kepler's imagination "makes the clothing and the flesh drop off, and the apparition of the naked skeleton of truth to stand revealed before him"[13]. For Peirce this marked Kepler as a path-breaker in the progressive "de-mythologization", of a world destined, in Max Weber's words, for general "disenchantment" through the operations of science: "we are not surprised", writes Peirce, "to find that Kepler looked on life with an eye of sadness, without tears, yet without illusion"[14].

The diagram, then, as the instrument of reasoning, is also an icon of modernity?

Yes, if, it has to be said, by "modernity" we mean to include all of the forms of thought stemming from what Husserl termed "Origin of Geometry", from Thalès, Anaximander, and, of course, Plato in the *Timaeus*. But it is also true that the self-consciousness of "disenchantment" emerging in the late 19th century, was an especially modern phenomenon as we might use the term.

And yet Peirce also holds out the promise that the diagram might lead toward another kind of future than that necessarily planned out by it?

Indeed. Because the diagram, unlike the expressive drawing, provides no depth of meaning beyond its surface—what Gilles Deleuze calls "insight" into its object—and as it, in itself, displays the formal features of its object, it substitutes for and takes the place of its object. This is why Peirce sees the diagram in some was eliding "the distinction between the real and the copy" a distinction which, Peirce claims, disappears entirely in the diagram. Here it is that the diagram reveals its fundamental link to utopia. The question it raises: is it a real object or is it a copy of a real object, makes it an instrument of suspended reality. As Peirce concludes: "It is, for the moment", he concludes, "a pure dream"[15]. Or, in other terms, the diagram may be seen as an instrument of and for utopia.

But then, is there any distinction to be drawn, historically, between diagrams in general, and specifically modern *diagrams?*

Yes: and here the contribution of Michel Foucault is critical. For it is Foucault who enters the diagram into the epistemological distinction between "classical" and "modern", into that "gap" or "break" which he finds so intriguing between the representation of traditional power and the signs of modern power. Indeed, it is the very presence of the diagram that demonstrates the existence of a new order of powers, and a new shape of institutions. In Foucault, the diagram is the icon of an epistemological shift. Hence the celebrated example of Bentham's Panopticon, for Foucault less an architectural project than an icon of "panopticism", the generalized dissemination of modern power through the optical and spatial mechanisms of surveillance.

But wasn't the form of the Panopticon, with its radially planned cells encircling a central observation post, simply an up-dating of every circular utopia since Plato's idealized models of Athens, Vitruvius's City of the Winds, and all the Renaissance utopias from Filarete on? What makes this especially "modern"?

Of course, all utopias are in some sense diagrams, and their diagrams are more or less all "perfectly closed in on themselves", often circular, and all geometrical. But the difference, say, between Filarete's Sforzinda and Bentham's Panopticon, is that the diagram of Sforzinda, with its squares rotated within a circle, is as much a *symbol* of its perfection, in harmony with the Platonic cosmos, as it is an *icon* of relationships. Bentham's Panopticon, by contrast, is the opposite of what Foucault calls "a dream building": "it is the diagram of a mechanism of power reduced to its ideal form". As such, it is an abstraction of its functioning—a "pure architectural and optical system" that recognizes no obstacle, resistance or friction in its operation. Its diagrammatic nature, indeed, "detached from any specific use"—Bentham suggested the plan for prisons, asylums, hospitals, workshops, and schools—allows it to become a "figure of political technology"[16].

But the Panopticon is only one example of eighteenth-century ideal planning. How is it to be considered a generalized figure?

Because, in Foucault's terms, all institutions at the end of the eighteenth century are undergoing a similar transformation, and, if they were not already in existence, were being developed according to the same schemata. A host—Foucault uses the word "swarming"—of new institutions were being invented in order to develop the disciplining, in the most general sense, of society; its "reform" according to rational principles as the *philosophies* put it. And of course Bentham was the very type of reformer—his prison was invented to redeem the criminal, re-fabricated (re-manufactured) in order to return to civil society; it was also, following Beccaria, an institution of temporal incarceration to replace torture and slave deportation as a civilized form of punishment. These institutions were not necessarily designed by architects, but by doctors, lawyers, scientists, educators, and not according to the laws of classical representation, but according to the rule of the diagram. This produced the first glimmerings of a "functional" architecture—"an architecture that is no longer built simply to be seen... but to permit an internal, articulated, and detailed control"[17].

But the discourse of power might have been right for the mid-sixties and seventies, but hasn't worn out its welcome thirty years on? What use is the panoptical diagram to us now?

It was Deleuze, who, precisely in his study of Foucault, who adumbrated a theory of the diagram that was at once more generalized and more evolutionary, if one can use that word, than in Foucault's own, historically specific, example. For Deleuze, Foucault's contribution was to have identified what he termed the "cartographic" character of the diagram. For Deleuze, the panoptical diagram generalized, was the specific prison diagram generalized to an entire society: "It is the map, it is cartography coextensive with the entire social field"[18]. For Deleuze the importance of the diagram is that it "specifies" in a particular way the relations between unformed/unorganized matter and unformalized/unfinalized functions, that it joins the two powerful regimes of space (the visible) and language

House III

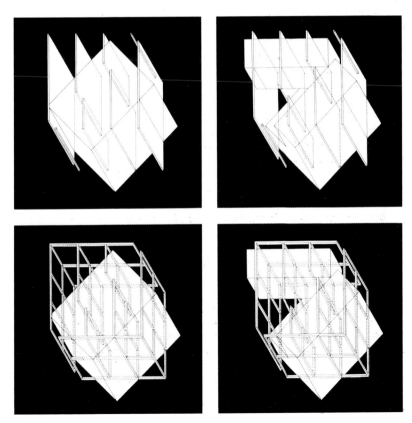

(the invisible but ubiquitous system). The *diagram*, then, in Deleuze's terms is a kind of map/machine, a spatio-temporal abstraction that "refuses every formal distinction between a content and an expression, between a discursive and a non-discursive formation. It is, he writes, "an almost silent/dumb and blind machine, even though it is that which causes sight and speech": "If there are many diagrammatic functions and even materials, it is because every diagram is a spatio-temporal multiplicity. But it is also because there are as many diagrams as there are social fields in history. When Foucault invokes the notion of the diagram, it is relation with our modern disciplinary societies, where power divides up the entire field in a grid: if there is a model for this, it is the model of the "plague" that sections off the ill city and extends into the smallest detail. There are accordingly diagrams for all social orders—for factories, theaters, monarchies, imperial regimes".

This, however, is simply to restate Foucault—what does Deleuze draw from this for his own philosophy?

We have to remember that all of Deleuze's re-readings of philosophers —Kant, Bergson, Nietzsche, Foucault—are in effect re-formulations; like the diagrams of which he speaks endlessly, previous philosophical maps are there to be re-drawn, their boundaries erased and their topographies disturbed. Here the diagram works hard: "What is more these diagrams are all interrelated—they interpenetrate each other. This is because the diagram is profoundly unstable or fluid, never ceasing to churn up matter and functions in such a way as to constitute mutations. Finally, every diagram is intersocial and in a state of becoming".

Then what happened to institutions in the late eighteenth century could happen again, with new and improved diagrams?

Not only that, it has already happened many times—first with Kant, then with Bergson, then with Foucault himself, who was, as we know hardly delineating diagrams for history's sake, but rather for his active politics of engagement with the late version of the carceral society in which he lived. Thus for Deleuze, the diagram's importance is that "it never functions to represent a preexisting world, it produces a new type of reality, a new model of truth. It is not subject to history, nor does it hang over history. It creates history by unmaking preceding realities and significations, setting up so many points of emergence or creativity, of unexpected conjunctures, of improbable continuums. It doubles history with a becoming [avec un devenir][19].

But what about Guattari—is he a diagram philosopher too?

It is this potential of mutation, of endless transformation and becoming, that makes the diagram for Deleuze, as well as Guattari, an especially transgressive device. As Gary Genosko has recently noted, the very fact that the diagram organizes an escape from pure linguistics into a deterritorialized spatial zone: "Diagrammatic machines of signs elude the territorializing systems of symbolic and signifying semiologies by displaying a kind of reserve in relation to their referents, forgoing polysemy and eschewing lateral signifying effects"[20]. This is why Guattari spends his life diagramming, dividing the world into flows and striations, orders and chaos. Diagrams are naturally and delightfully ill-behaved, they "do not behave like well-formed signs in a universal system of signification and fail to pass smoothly through the simulacral dialogism of ideal models of communication"[21]. In this way, what might seem to be "an arid algebra of language" in diagram form actively serves Guattari's "pragmatics of the unconscious" and thence his insurgent social practice[22].

The panopticon gives us an insight into the emergence of the functionalist diagram, and we can trace its influence throughout the modern movement, and well into the architectural practice of the late twentieth century. But if we are as critics engaged in a insurgent social practice, how does the diagram help us in developing an insurgent architectural practice? Isn't the diagram as we know it now simply the icon of corporate economics?

Of course, as Peirce indicated, and Foucault and Deleuze sustained, there is nothing ontological about the diagram—it declares itself for or against nothing. But the development of a critical diagram is as potentially de-stabilising to convention as the sustenance of a normative diagram. Deleuze, in his study of the painter Francis Bacon, finds that in the painter's practice—in the literal application of paint to the canvas—the diagram (or "graph" as Bacon calls it) is several times disturbed, erased, and re-construed. The mental graph of the painter is in this way directly obliterated by the act of painting. The "figurative givens" whether in the painter's head or on the canvas, will be "removed by the act of painting", wiped out, erased, covered over[23]. Such a process, that sees the diagram as something to be mutilated and recreated, scored, and re-scored by the marks of the hand, might indicate a parallel practice for architecture.

But surely you are not saying that we should return to the time of chiaroscuro, of clair-obscur, of patina, and intuition?

This would, even if desired, be impossible—only the simulacra would remain. But such a practice of erasure can easily be envisaged with respect to the analytical drawing, whether constructed by hand or digitally. Look for example at Eisenman's Terragni drawings. It is not clear to me that all the elaborate, analytical decosntructions of the Casa del Fascio are in themselves diagrams, properly speaking. Each one is too specific to perform this role. But it is clear that Eisenman possesses a "diagram" of Terragni, or that, so to speak, "Terragni" is a diagram for Eisenman. Rather in the same way that the Dom-ino house is a diagram for Le Corbusier, and all his ensuing villas are elaborations of this diagram, as well as its erasure—with their own diagrams to be sure, so that the villas are in effect diagrams of diagrams—so for Eisenman, Terragni holds a diagram, envisaged as a mental cartography of formal relations, that underlies each of the individual investigations. *Diagram Diaries* is, in this sense, a record of the search for a diagram that, precisely because it is a diagram can never be entirely constituted as such, but acts as a spur to the genetic production of subsidiary diagrams, new diagrams that take as their elements old diagrams, and so on. The endless permutations, and all those that might be imagined but are not there, do not in themselves define, or pin down the diagram. Rather they establish a kind of rhythm of enquiry, a punctual relationship between

"Terragni" and "Eisenman" over a lifetime. And in this process, the diagram emerges as the icon of catastrophe, of its own obliteration. As Deleuze notes of Pollock: "the painting thus becomes catastrophe painting and a diagram painting at one and the same time"[24].

Yet Eisenman has hardly ever referred to Deleuze, while he has often, at least since 1985, claimed Derrida as a strong influence. What would a diagram be for Derrida?

It's not at all clear that Derrida would have proposed the "diagram" as a model of thought; at first sight one might understand deconstruction as a thoroughgoing destruction of all iconic signs. And yet, given Freud's propensity for diagramming the "architecture of the unconscious", and Derrida's fascination with the idea of the "mysic writing pad", and its "traces", one might begin to discern a consistent preoccupation with a certain kind of mental diagram in Derrida. This might be, for example, connected to the network set up by the ambiguous or polysemic meanings ascribed by words—such as the *pharmakon*, or the *chôra*—, words that far from delineating precision, describe a field of operation, within and outside of a text. The very impossibility of pinning such words down, the demand for all texts to be undone as positive signs or instruments of meaning, would in this sense be a diagram. Perhaps here, the affinity Derrida/Eisenman might be characterized as a practice based on the *mental* maps, of which Peirce speaks, but one that never resolves itself into fixed or purely iconic signs.

Does this mean that the "diagram" is everything or nothing, in the same sense indicated by Derrida's chôra?

Not entirely, although the status of neither this/nor that does allow for a certain diagrammatic productivity built up on the interference—what Norbert Wiener would call "noise" of the oscillation between the two poles. And mention of Norbert Wiener, returns us to the domain of semiology, but in the manner of information theory, of cybernetics, as developed after the Second World War.

But this would be to open up an entirely different domain of discussion—that of cybernetic diagrams as the progenitors of digital diagrams. Might we say that the notion of feedback is in a sense built into the diagram from the outset?

Yes, and what is remarkable about the development of digital diagrams in the last decades, is the extent to which they depend on information and communication theory, and even more, to which they reveal the processes working behind the diagram itself. Indeed, software iteration, linked to the input of certain information, when animated, provides a map that is neither quite "mental" nor purely iconic, a map that can be manipulated at will to produce other maps.

The circle is thus closed: from Peirce to Deleuze a theory of the diagram has evolved to the extent that it is enacted on the screen. This is at once the delight of diagrammatic play, and the trap of facility; when diagrams had to be laboriously engraved, delineated, and drawn by hand their ubiquity was controlled by thought. With digital iteration, diagrams become both malleable and potentially thoughtless. The control of diagrams—

their policing—will become for the next decade the central question of theory: not what would thinking about diagrams mean, but in what way might diagrams think?

Which would return us to Derrida, and his often asked question", the question of architecture as a possibility of thought, which cannot be reduced to the status of a representation of thought"[25]. We might ask precisely the same question of the architectural diagram, about diagrammatic thinking.

[1] *The Compact Edition of the Oxford English Dictionary*, vol. 1 (OUP, 1971), p. 714.

[2] Ch.S. Peirce, *The Essential Peirce. Selected Philosophical Writings*, vol. 2 (1893-1913), p. 13.

[3] *Ibid.*

[4] *Ibid.*, p. 14.

[5] *Ibid.*, p. 17.

[6] *Ibid.*, p. 274.

[7] *Ibid.*, p. 13.

[8] *Ibid.*, pp. 206-207.

[9] *Ibid.*, p. 212.

[10] *Ibid.*

[11] *Ibid.*, pp. 246-247

[12] *Ibid.*, pp. 206-207

[13] Ch.S. Peirce, *Values in a Universe of Chance. Selected Writings of Charles S. Peirce (1839-1914)*, edited with an Introduction and Notes by P.P. Wiener, Doubleday, New York, 1958, p. 255, essay on "Kepler".

[14] *Ibid.*

[15] *Ibid.*

[16] M. Foucault, *Discipline and Punish. The Birth of the Prison*, trans. Alan Sheridan, Allen Lane, London, 1977, p. 205.

[17] *Ibid.*, p. 172.

[18] G. Deleuze, *Foucault*, Editions Minuit, Paris, 1985, p. 42.

[19] *Ibid.*, p. 43.

[20] G. Genosko, "Guattari's Schizoanalytic Semiotics", in E. Kaufman and K.J. Heller, eds., *Deleuze and Guattari. New Mappings in Politics, Philosophy, and Culture*, University of Minnesota Press, Minneapolis, 1998, pp. 175-190.

[21] *Ibid.*, p. 186.

[22] *Ibid.*, p. 175.

[23] G. Deleuze, *Francis Bacon, The Logic of Sensation*, trans. Daniel W. Smith, Afterword by Tom Conley, University of Minnesota Press, Minneapolis, 2003, p. 81.

[24] *Ibid.*, p. 86.

[25] J. Derrida, "Architecture Where the Desire May Live," interview with Eva Meyer, *Domus*, vol. 67 (1986), p. 17.

Critical Analyses

Toward an Understanding of Form in Architecture

Two contemporary English critics have put forward certain ideas on the theory of modern architecture. By doing so they have raised between them the problem of form in architecture and provided the bases for taking it to a subsequent phase.

In a lecture at the Royal Institute of British Architects in May 1961, Sir John Summerson suggests two possible ways of resolving our problems, one of which concerns the notion of fundamental solids as the basis of form in architecture. Summerson begins as follows: "Imagine just for a moment the task of isolating by characteristics the modern forms from the globality of buildings". Then he goes on to say that "on this principle of geometric absoluteness, it is possible to construct systems or disciplines that allow the architect to be guided toward that order of the form that he must reach".

In contrast, Reyner Banham, in his book *Theory and Design of the First Machine Age*, would seem to deny the possibility of establishing any principle that is based on considerations on form, and discusses the validity of the Corbusierian equation on the norms of Phileban solids with the principles that govern the universe.

In this article I am not attempting to isolate "modern" forms, nor to propose a joint system for criticism and project work. I will restrict myself to presenting some ideas that may help clarify the relationships that form has in all architectures. One of my theses will be to affirm that formal considerations are fundamental to any architecture, irrespective of the style, and that these by themselves can help us develop a language agreed upon both for criticism and for project work, the detailed nature of which, its grammar and its syntax, will not be considered for reasons of space. My observations proceed by prolegomena; they do not fill the evident void in contemporary architectural thought, but they will at least serve to denote its existence. Initially the essence of every creative act can be thought of as communication of an original idea of the author to the person who receives it via an expressive means. And the expressive means must be such as to transmit the original intention as clearly and completely as possible to the person who receives it. This need for clarity and comprehensibility, much requested by Gestalt psychologists, is crucial for the development of any means of communication. Elements such as scale, harmony, model, etc. should first be conceived as useful elements with regard to the comprehensibility of expression. Formal order, therefore, cannot be considered as an end in itself, but as useful for clarification purposes.

Architecture can be linked to various elements to transmit its total meaning and to produce the final result, that is to say, a building, a group of buildings or a total environment. All these elements contribute to defining the architectural equation, and I will define them as concept, or intention, function, structure, technique, form. It will be obvious, I think, as soon as we come to examine them, that they are not of equal importance or scope. From some passages by Choisy, it would seem that architecture should be divulged by technicians. Other theorists of the 19th century, including Louis Sullivan, would have claimed that architecture is in the first instance the manifestation of function. The first modern theorists have been typically inclined toward a sociological and historicist position, as emerges from their talking of architecture as an expression of "the spirit of the age" or "the will of the age", thus preferring the element of the intention. Yet what none of these theorists has attempted has been to define exactly what the term they use means, and to what point form is useful or dominant among the elements listed. This partial ordering cannot by itself provide a rational discipline for architecture, and it becomes dangerous when it is used in a volitive or capricious way in the project process. The uncoordinated or non-rational invoking of this or that other element is one of the first causes of the architectural confusion that we are often faced with.

Not that the problem is easily resolvable; for example, the indications of form are not always totally reconcilable with the requirements of function; and also, a function that appears as symbolic to one particular culture may seem utilitarian to another. This does not imply that the elements named are by their very nature antagonistic, but rather that, when they are weighed equally, their identities are lost so that the effect of the building from which they result is inevitably invalidated. Consequently, conceiving a rational hierarchy of elements ends up being a necessary precondition for the solution, and effectively even for a clear formulation of an architectural problem. Such a hierarchy could derive from both the general and the particular requirement set by the problem. In other words, in architecture we must establish a basic priority to evolve from the dialectic between relative and absolute finalities. Such a proposal is of crucial importance today, since our social, economic and technological environment has been so dilated as to ensure that no single individual can perceive any type of order in it. Furthermore, the proliferation of new technological instruments has evolved beyond any capacity that architects may have to use their potentiality rationally. In this situation, architecture seems to take refuge in mannerism and in the cult of self-expressiveness, in a compulsive emphasis on isolated creation without any total order. This need for an individual expressiveness is legitimate, but if it must be satisfied without any prejudice to the comprehensibility of the environment conceived as total, it is necessary to propose a system of general priorities and it will be shown here that this system must necessarily prefer absolute to temporal finalities.

If we suppose the general situation, that is, the total external order, as our absolute order, then it follows that a specific situation, by its very nature, restricts us within relative finalities. This is equivalent to stating that we currently see the individual building as a relative goal in relation to its environment. The individual building cannot be seen as an isolated entity, as an end in itself, but simply as an element of transition in the completion of the whole. It can still take on a condition of "ideality" that is integral in itself, but only within the limits imposed by the envisaged future order.

In pragmatic terms, it is clearly impossible to create a specific building with a finality or an absolute end in sight, because every new unit will not only modify the existing model, but will also modify with its presence every future model that results from the addition of other units. In considering a building, for example, we cannot locate its entrances where no means of access exists to material time. To this end, every building must recognize the existence of external models, inasmuch as these could be considered as parts of a future absolute order. To complicate this problem still further, any future order cannot be a static or constant entity, but must be conceived as continuous and capable of accepting growth and mutations. Any notion of future order, in strictly static terms, would be criticized as romantic and utopian. The designs of Sant'Elia for a "new city" are significant examples of this type of visionary approach. For Sant'Elia futurist notions of energy and speed were absolutes for which he sought an architectural expression. But in doing so, he involved

himself in an essential contradiction, since the buildings he designed, being necessarily specific and relative, could only presuppose a relative and mutable future condition. He imposed aerodynamic and tapered aesthetics on these designs, making them symbolic of the futurist utopia. Irrespective of how much the effect of these images could be stimulating, they are of no help to any realistic reflection on the problem of the future continuous model, nor to a rational approach that must spread a total order, or, in the terms I have used, to an absolute that is capable of including change and growth, yet conserving its own absoluteness. It is the concept of the priority of absolute ends that is critical here, since alone it can provide us with the basis for a hierarchical order of the five elements. This major task must now be attempted. It is my thesis that architecture is essentially giving form (itself an element) to intent, function, structure and technics, and in stating this I raise form to a position of primacy in the hierarchy of elements.

(Excerpted from P. Eisenman, Ph.D. Thesis, *The Formal Basis of Modern Architecture*, University of Cambridge, 1963.)

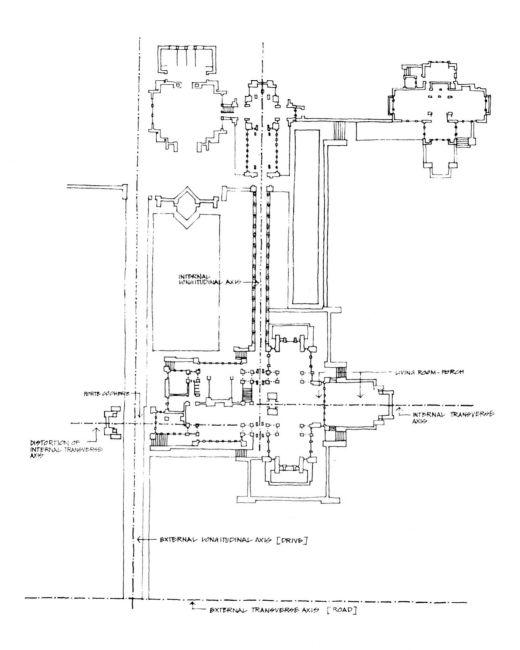

INTERNAL
LONGITUDINAL AXIS

LIVING ROOM - PORCH

PORTE COCHERE

INTERNAL TRANSVERSE
AXIS

DISTORTION OF
INTERNAL TRANSVERSE
AXIS

EXTERNAL LONGITUDINAL AXIS [DRIVE]

EXTERNAL TRANSVERSE AXIS [ROAD]

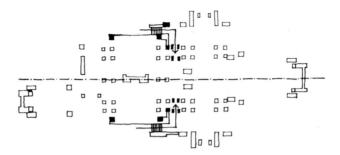

5.

EQUATION OF FRONT ENTRY WITH MINOR
REAR ENTRY EXPLAINS AWKWARD TERMINATION
OF ENTRY MOVEMENT. EMPHASIZES ENTRY
TO RECEPTION HALL .

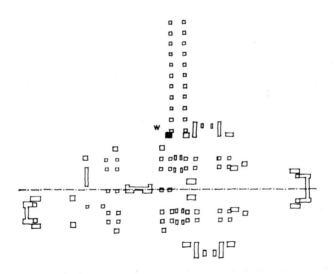

6.

PIER W NOT INVOLVED IN AN AXIAL
SYMMETRY ABOUT TRANSVERSE AXIS

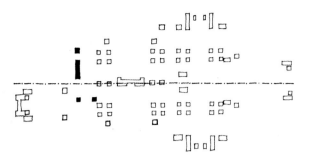

7.

ELEMENTS OF SERVANT'S DINING ROOM
LAVATORY, AND OFFICE NOT PART OF
SYMMETRICAL ORDER.

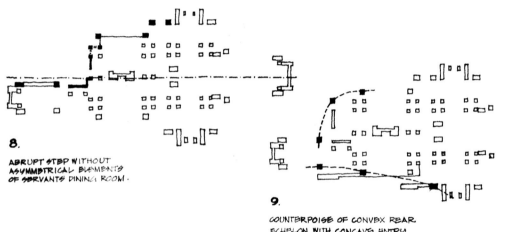

8.

ABRUPT STEP WITHOUT
ASYMMETRICAL ELEMENTS
OF SERVANTS DINING ROOM.

9.

COUNTERPOISE OF CONVEX REAR
ECHELON WITH CONCAVE ENTRY
ECHELON.

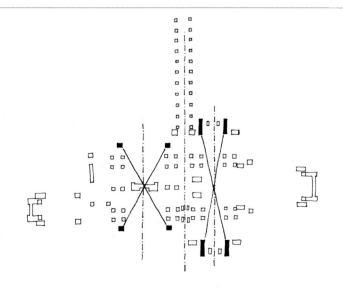

10.

DEVELOPMENT OF MINOR AXES
AND COUNTERPOISE OF VOLUMES
ABOUT LONGITUDINAL AXIS.

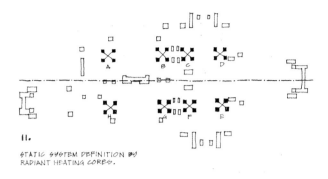

11.

STATIC SYSTEM DEFINITION BY
RADIANT HEATING CORES.

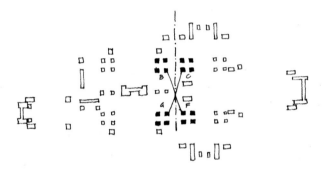

12.

DEFINITION TO DOMINANT
CENTRAL AXIS WHEN READ AS
BC AND FG

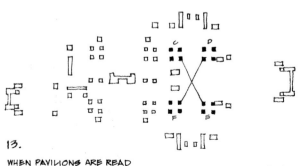

13.

WHEN PAVILIONS ARE READ
AS CD AND EF THEY DEFINE
THE LIVING ROOM. —

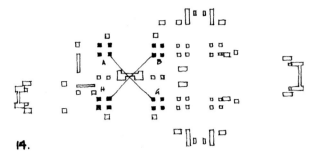

14.

-WHEN READ AS AB-GH THEY
DEFINE THE RECEPTION HALL-
KITCHEN VOLUME.

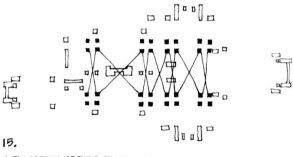

15.

A PULSATING SERIES OF STATIC
VOLUMES ABOUT THE TRANSVERSE
AXIS.

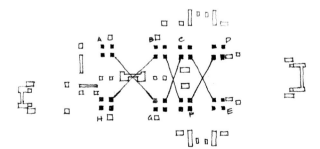

16.

CONTINUOUS READING OF
HEATING CORES AS ABGH
BCFG AND CDEF.

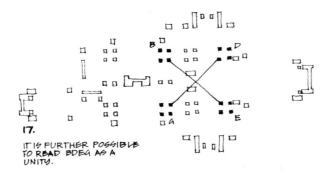

17.

IT IS FURTHER POSSIBLE
TO READ BDEG AS A
UNITY.

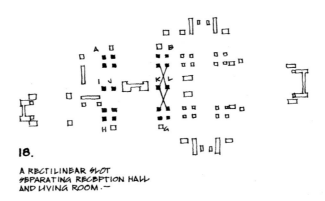

18.

A RECTILINEAR SLOT
SEPARATING RECEPTION HALL
AND LIVING ROOM.—

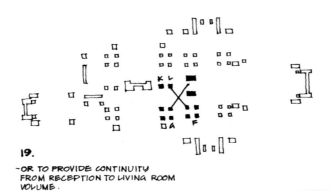

19.

—OR TO PROVIDE CONTINUITY
FROM RECEPTION TO LIVING ROOM
VOLUME.

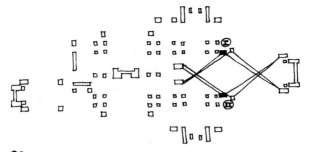

20.

CONTINUOUS READING OF LIVING ROOM
AND PORCH.

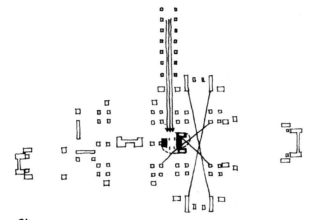

21.

AMBIGUITY OF LIVING ROOM
LOCATION REFLECTED IN
POSITION OF FIREPLACE.

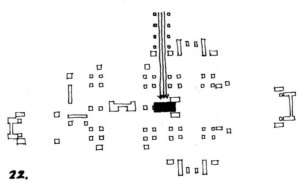

22.

FIREPLACE CONSIDERED
AS A CENTRAL CORE
SHATTERED BY PERGOLA VECTOR.

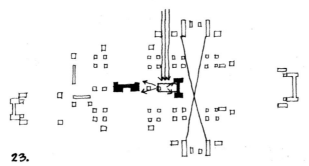

23.

LIVING ROOM HALF OF CORE
TURNED INTO LONGITUDINAL POSITION
BECAUSE OF LIVING ROOM ROTATION.

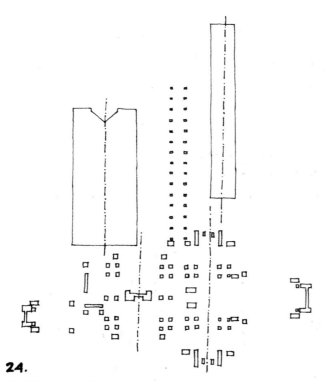

24.

STUTTERING OF INTERNAL
AND EXTERNAL AXIS TO
PREVENT ANY CONFUSION
WITH MAJOR AXIAL REFERENCES.

A Critical Analysis: Giovan Battista Piranesi

One of the most powerful ideas that Jacques Derrida addresses in *Of Grammatology* is the possibility of another form of memory, a memory that no longer deals with fragments or figuration or abstraction but with something he calls the "trace". The trace is the presence of an absence, a presence no longer in its metaphysical fullness nor an absence as a dialectical opposite to presence, but rather something that exceeds the dialectic. It is more like a non-absent absence. But a memory trace is not new to architecture.

One of the best examples of the memory trace exists in architecture in one of G.B. Piranesi's didactic maps of the Campo Marzio, drawn in 1762. To understand the idea of trace, Piranesi's drawing must be compared to the Nolli plan of Rome. Drawn in 1748, the Nolli plan has today become the icon of an architectural fundamentalism which calls itself New Urbanism. It represents an idea of original truth, of a moment in time that uses this moment in the eighteenth century as a badge of authenticity to authorize work in the present. The Nolli map was a literal projection of Rome as it was in the eighteenth century. On the other hand, the Campo Marzio has little to do with representing a literal place or an actual time. The Campo Marzio is a fabric of traces, a weaving of fact and fiction.

The traces of the Campo Marzio have nothing to do with a literal representation of space and time as an aesthetic image; rather, they project time and space as well as act as an index of both. Piranesi uses the Rome that was extant in the eighteenth century as a starting point, but that possesses no original value; it is merely a being in the present. From this existential moment of being, he takes buildings that existed in the first and second centuries, in Imperial Rome, and places them in the same framework of time and space as the eighteenth-century city. Next, Piranesi moves monuments of the first century from their actual location to other locations, as if these were their actual sites again in the eighteenth century. Piranesi also draws in buildings that never existed. They seem at first glance to be memories of buildings that could have existed; they look like buildings until one examines them as functioning buildings. This idea of a building as a trace of function is similar to Piranesi's project for the Colegio Romano, which has a seemingly centralized plan. However, when it is analyzed, it does not actually function; it only symbolizes its function.

Equally, the Campo Marzio would not function as an urban entity. There are no streets as such; rather, the ground is filled with what can be called interstitial figures. In this fabric of fact and fiction, there are no clear figure/ground relationships, one of the underpinnings of the dialectics of contemporary architecture. There is no primacy given to the ground or to the figure. The result is not a figure/ground projection, as in the Nolli map, but what could be called a figure/figure urbanism. This idea of urbanism does not give primacy to the ground as an original instance or datum. Rather, the ground becomes an interstitial trace between objects, which are also traces in both in time and space. This presents a theoretical basis for urbanism as a tissue of memory rather than as a nostalgia for static icons. Such a notion is close to what Charles Sanders Peirce calls an index. In this context, an index can be considered as a record of events; it is a notational matrix. It undercuts all metaphysical ideas of truth and ideality. It is a multiple palimpsest, a series of overlays that mix fact with fiction.

(Excerpted from P. Eisenman, "Notations of Affect", in Klaus Herding and Bernhard Stumpfhaus (eds.), *Pathos, Affekt, Gefühl: Die Emotionen in den Künsten*, Walter de Gruyter, Berlin, 2004.)

G.B. Piranesi,
Campo Marzio, 1762

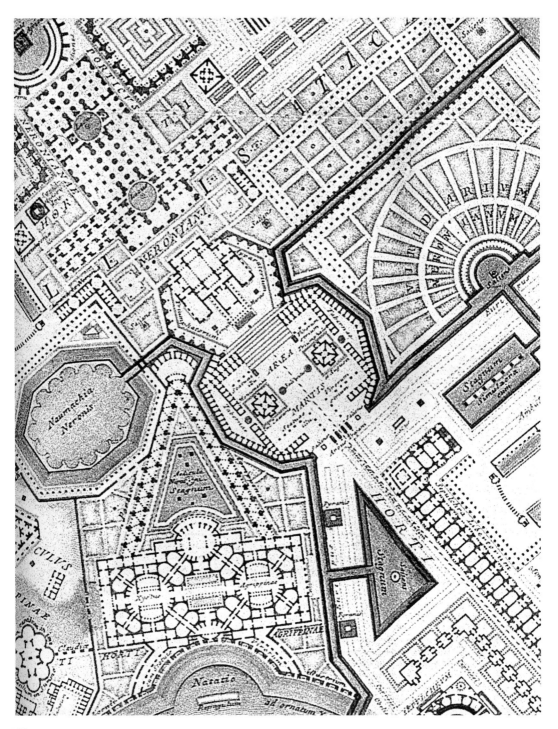

G.B. Piranesi,
Campo Marzio, 1762

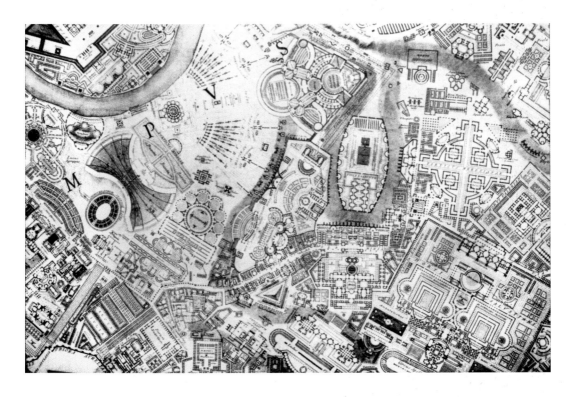

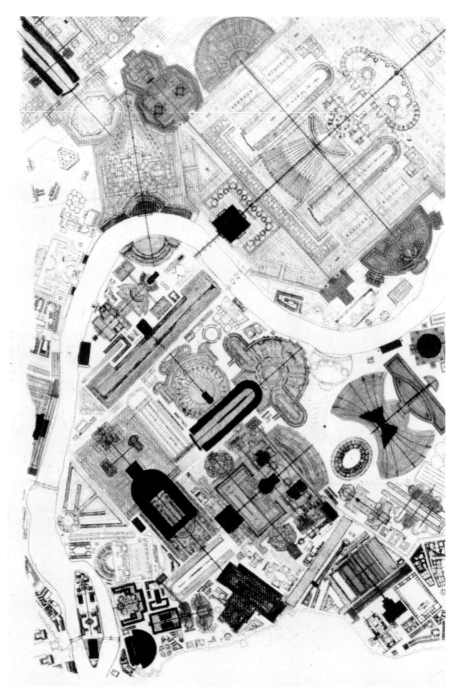

P. Eisenman and students.
Analyses of Campo Marzio

P. Eisenman and students.
Analyses of Campo Marzio

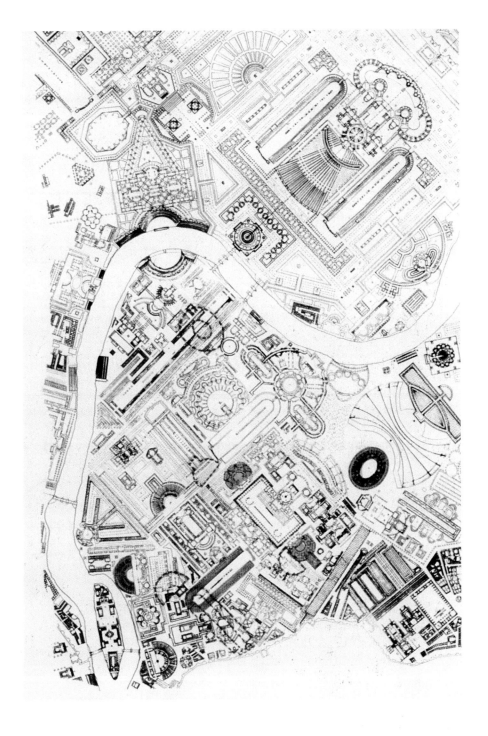

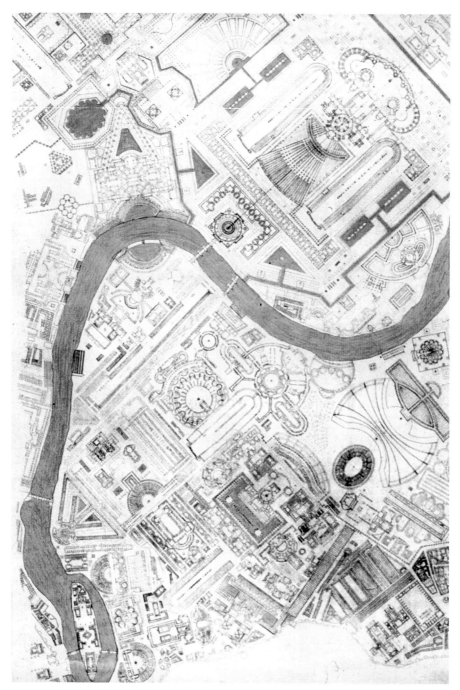

P. Eisenman and students.
Analyses of Campo Marzio

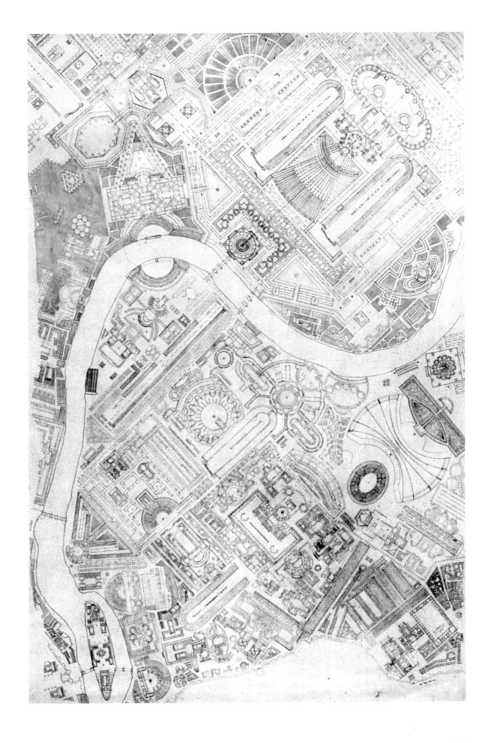

A Critical Analysis: Andrea Palladio

The invention of perspective as a system of representation in the fifteenth century may have been ultimately
a more decisive issue in architecture than it was in
painting. Perspective necessarily replaces a naïve, narrative representation of reality—three-dimensional objects disposed in space—by an internally coherent set
of graphic conventions which require a strictly controlled order. Indeed, architecture was an essential instrument for this kind of representation. In fact, more
significant paintings of the new perspective type in the
early fifteenth century employed architecture as their
convenient setting.

For, while this convention allowed painting to represent depth in space more naturally, it allowed architecture to represent deep space on a façade surface
and thus to become more like painting. In painting it
provided the illusion of reality; in architecture it reduced
real space to the illusion of flat space on the painted
surface. Thus perspective introduced into the built object both a connection to and a distinction between architecture and the image of architecture. The possibility now existed of the representation of space in architecture, that is, a representation of architecture by
architecture; now, rather than imitating "nature" in the
way that a Corinthian capital represents nature, architecture might itself be its own representation.

With the introduction of perspective, architecture
was no longer merely a form of reality itself, but also
imitated reality. The vertical plane as a surface for the
representation of deep space necessarily forced architecture to become both reality *and* representation. Perspective also forced an explicit change in the relationship of the viewer to the object, from sequential, linear time to time understood as a particular place. This
representation for the architects of the Renaissance
was always related to "natural" space. For them, perspective was considered a law of nature, not a representation of it. Perspective was the mediation between
man and nature, between what man sees and how he
sees. For Palladio perspective was artificial and not natural; it could be used to break apart the relationship between man and nature. For Palladio, man becomes the

new nature and perspective becomes transformed from
a state of nature to a tool of representation—a technique in relationship to man.

According to Giulio Argan, Palladio's architecture
does not set out to represent space, that is, to represent natural law, but rather to represent a system of
logical manufacture of absolute value apart from all
meaning[1]. The absolute value was architecture itself.
In Palladio, architecture thus rejects perspective and its
representation; it is in Argan's terms "non-perspec-
tive". For Palladio, the image becomes a sign, and the
sign is not so much a representation of something else
as it is a code for its own internal system. This introduced a second angle in the relationship between subject and object. Now the object has become the house
of man, not the house of nature. And when the object
becomes dwelling it begins to erode the traditional sub-
ject/object relationship. Thus Palladio was concerned
not so much with the representation of "natural" conditions of building, but more with this altered condition
of the object produced by the concept of perspective.

Palladio deliberately disconnects and disintegrates
the relationship to previous architecture. The destruction of these prior relationships produces the quality of
unrelatedness or absoluteness in the individual forms.
This destruction produces a third change between subject and object. Now, the flatness of a Palladian façade
is counter to the perspectival flatness of a canvas. This
produces an uncertainty as to the exact nature of the
object. Where previous architecture attempted to mirror the certainty of nature, Palladio's architecture mir-
rored this doubt over the status of the object.

(Excerpted from P. Eisenman, "The Representations of Doubt:
At the Sign of the Sign", in *Eisenman Inside Out: Selected
Writings 1963–1988*, Yale University Press, 2004. First pub-
lished in Italian in 1982.)

[1] G.C. Argan, "The Impor-
tance of Sanmicheli in the
Formation of Palladio", in *Re-
naissance Art*, ed. Creighton
Gilbert, Harper and Rowe,
New York, 1973, p. 173.

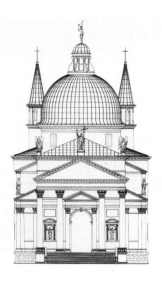

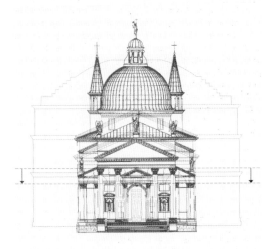

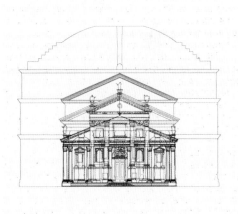

P. Eisenman, analytical
diagrams of the church
of the Redeemer, Venice

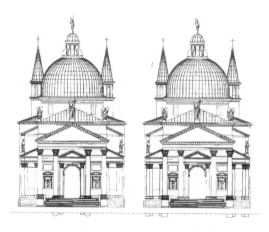

P. Eisenman, analytical
diagrams of the church
of the Redeemer, Venice

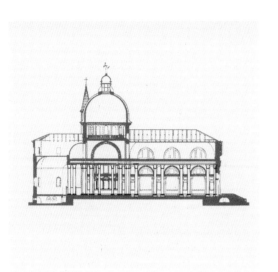

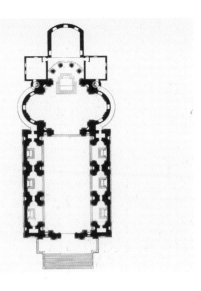

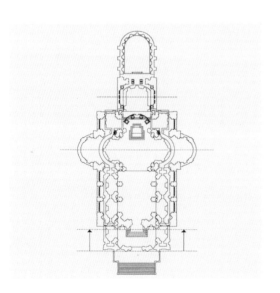

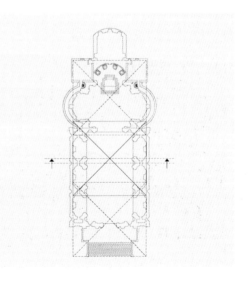

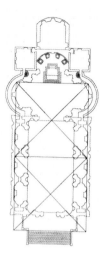
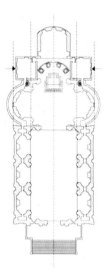
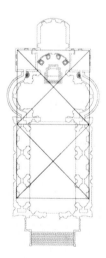
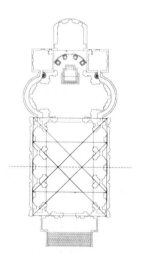

P. Eisenman, analytical
diagrams of the church
of the Redeemer, Venice

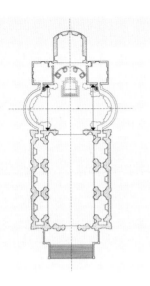

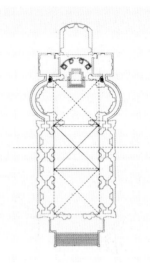

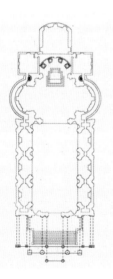

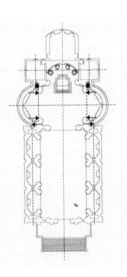

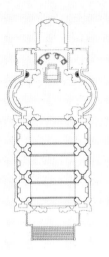
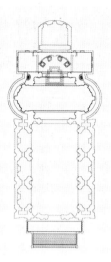
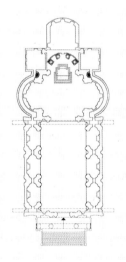
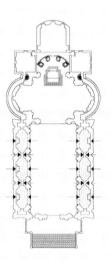

P. Eisenman, analytical
diagrams of the church
of the Redeemer, Venice

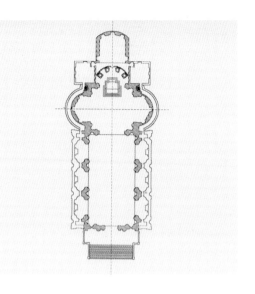

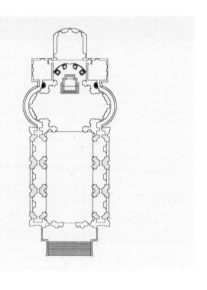

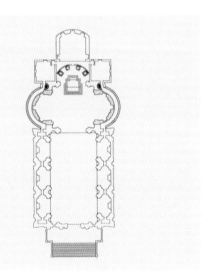

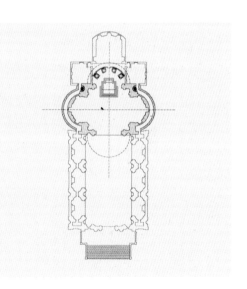

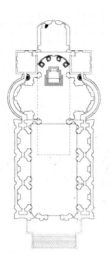
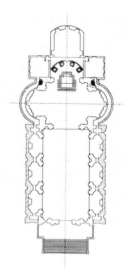

P. Eisenman, analytical
diagrams of the church
of the Redeemer, Venice

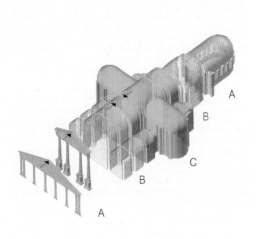

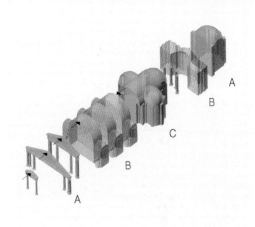

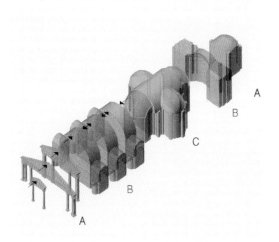

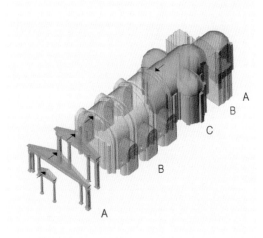

P. Eisenman, exploded
axonometric view of the
church of the Redeemer,
Venice

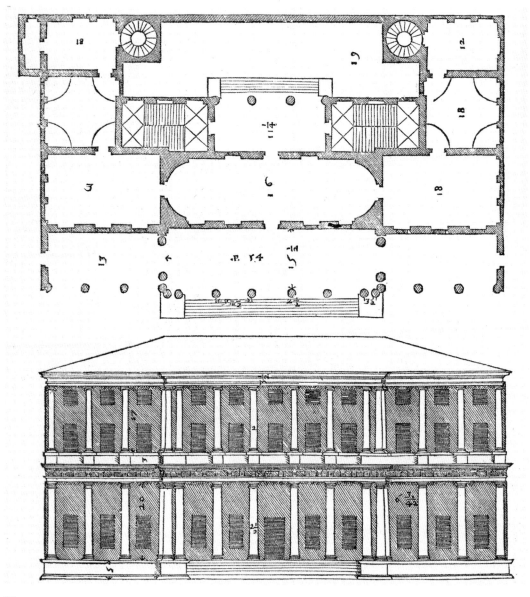

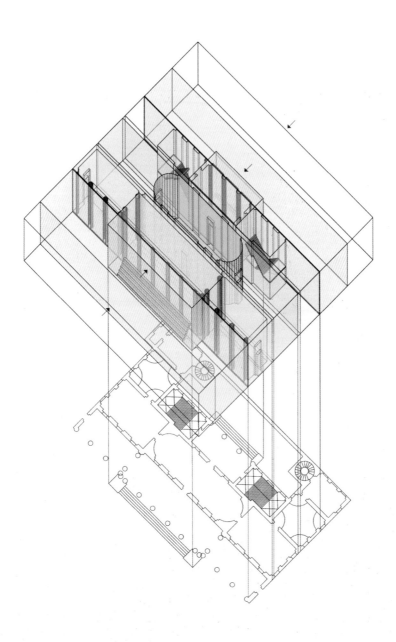

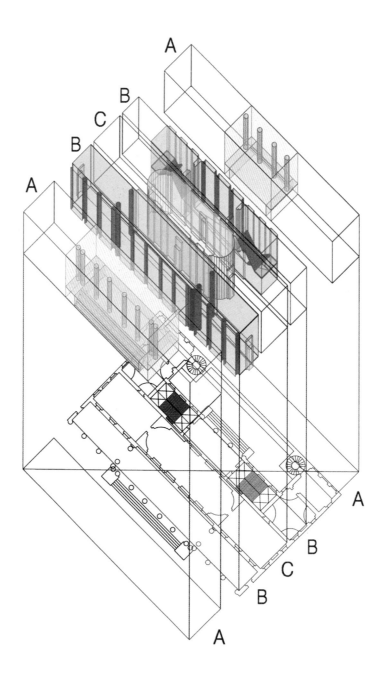

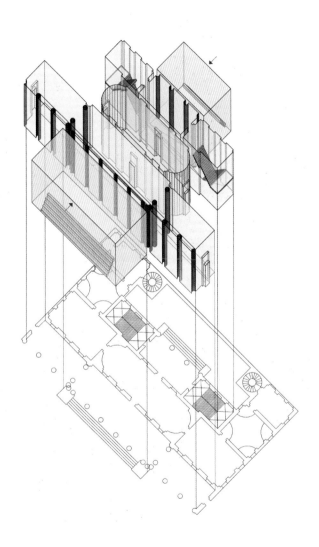

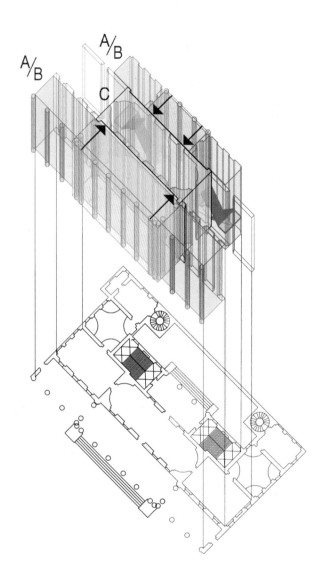

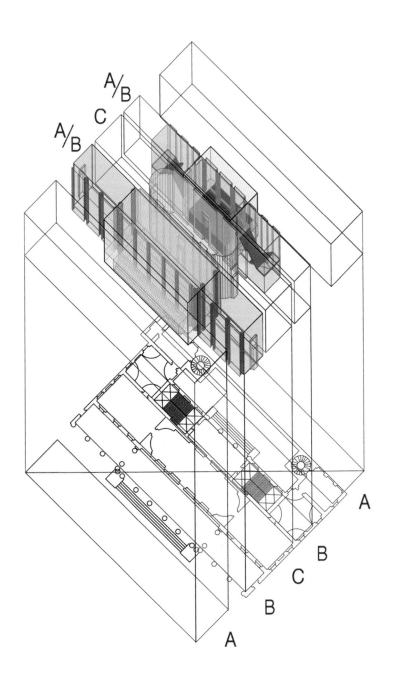

A/B

A/B

C

A

B

C

B

A

A Critical Analysis: Luigi Moretti

Luigi Moretti's Casa del Girasole in Rome sits on a rectangular block bounded by two major streets, a minor one, and a service road. This block is cut in two through most of its center, creating an essentially U-shaped condition from front to back and from street level to the roof. On its upper three residential floors, its two long sides are splayed by three minor cuts, as an axe cuts into a block of wood. The central void gives the initial appearance of an axial symmetry, which is belied in the actual configuration of the side blocks, which are not parallel to each other. While the front façade is orthogonal to the main street, viale Bruno Buozzi, the rear façade volume is parallel to its street but at a slight angle to the front façade. This creates a cranked condition on what would be an axis of symmetry, and a wracking of the rightmost block off of the 90-degree corner made by the intersection of viale Bruno Buozzi and via Schiaparelli. In addition, both the front and back façade planes extend beyond their building masses, while the typical floor plans have a central void containing a main stair and elevator, and a service stair and elevator in the rear.

Moretti's work deals with several issues that seem to question modernist abstraction as a basis. One is called, in Italian, modanatura. Modanatura is the idea of profile. In modern architecture there was no profile. While there were columns, walls, and façades, these were usually related in such a way as to eliminate any profile. Profile is how a surface in architecture meets space, both inside and outside. It is an idea that comes out of the history of architecture and distinguishes architecture from painting. In painting there is a frame for an object, or an edge of an object, that does not exist in real space and time. It only exists in illustrative or representational space and time. In painting, a profile is a line. In architecture, a profile is the edge of a plane or the edge of a surface. It is also the edge of either the containing surface or the edge of the exterior space in relationship to the containing surface of the interior.

Potentially more important than the idea of modanatura is the series of models built by Moretti, which still stand today as canonical early postmodern works. These models were published in Moretti's magazine "Spazio". The title itself was interesting because it could be understood to be making a distinction between the object, that is, the thing, and the thing being contained, that is, space. This is important because a thing can be seen and analyzed in abstraction. Space, on the other hand, is difficult to analyze as an abstract entity because it is undefined in itself; it is always defined by other things.

In the history of architecture, analysis usually begins from the geometrical—that is, from those things that you can touch and define metaphysically, like structure, walls, etc.—and then moves to a spatial analysis, which deals with that which is contained within physical boundaries. The movement between object, or geometry, and space defines the history of architecture.

Moretti's models represent the volumes of the space of a series of buildings without their surfaces.

L. Moretti, Casa del Girasole, Rome, axonometry and elevations

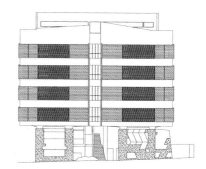

They take space as a dominant characteristic as opposed to surface. The modeling of the space itself becomes the primary condition of being. On one hand, Moretti deals with the edge of surface—its profile—but on the other, he deals with volume without surface.

A third issue that comes with the modeling of space and modanatura is the casting of shadows. Profiles cast shadows. Moretti introduces in the effects of his architecture strategies that are deployed in the making of profile, or space, to generate the possibility of affects, which are shadows. Shadowing allows space that is not merely abstract space, space that is open to formal analysis, but space that is open to an affective response. The black and white films, especially those made in the late 1940s and early 1950s, have harsh shadows cast by very bright light.

In the Casa del Girasole itself, materiality replaces abstraction. The materials do not stand for anything; they do not represent anything; they are. At the same time, there is no dominant material system that suggests a preference for one material over another. Neither is there a color palette that makes any kind of structural or formal sense; the colors merely exist. This is a form of neorealism in architecture.

All of the elements refer back and forth to one another. No single material is dominant, but rather a series of materials articulate their differences. Rather than being monolithic, they become parts of a construct, which is only whole in a literal, material sense but not as an idea.

The fundamental difference between a formal analysis and a textual analysis in architecture lies in the idea of the metaphysics of presence. Formal analysis assumes as a truth the premise that architecture is the locus of the metaphysics of presence, while a textual analysis begins to question this assumption, going beyond the dialectics of form/function, figure/ground, public/private, which are grounded in such a metaphysics.

A formal analysis pretends to begin from an internal logic that is linear and narrative, beginning from an initial idea or diagram. Textual analysis suspends narrative and hierarchy. In a text, there is not one truth but many truths; not one diagram, but a series of diagrams. A formal analysis is basically a narrative; a text is a tissue of traces that denies narrative. A text is a web; a narrative is a string. A textual analysis attempts to look at material without saying there is any particular truth, or any particular value, to one thread more than the other.

In structuralism and formalism, structure is the dominant idea. In postmodernism, the fragment becomes a textual integer. Architecture will always be presence, and therefore the assumption of its metaphysic. In order to question the status of presence, the foundation of much of architecture's basis since the Renaissance, it is necessary to displace concepts which have become conventionalized, such as place, meaning, function, and the like. This questioning is the essence of criticality.

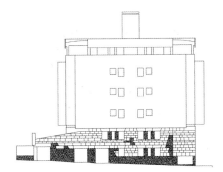

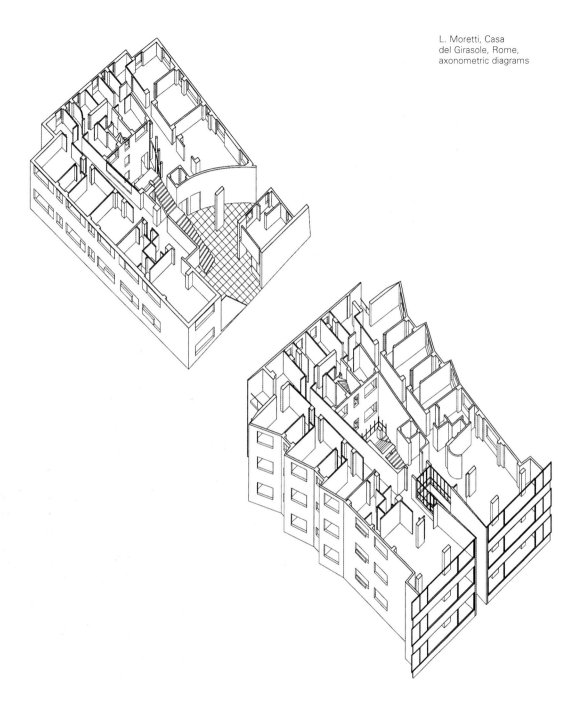

L. Moretti, Casa
del Girasole, Rome,
axonometric diagrams

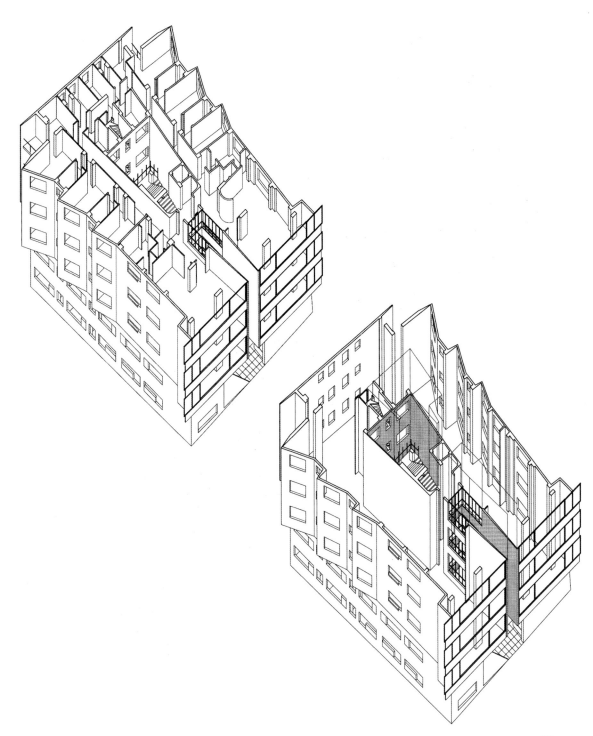

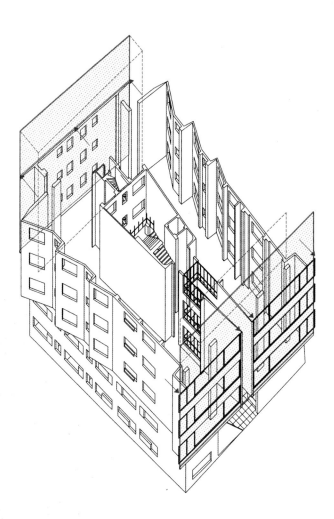

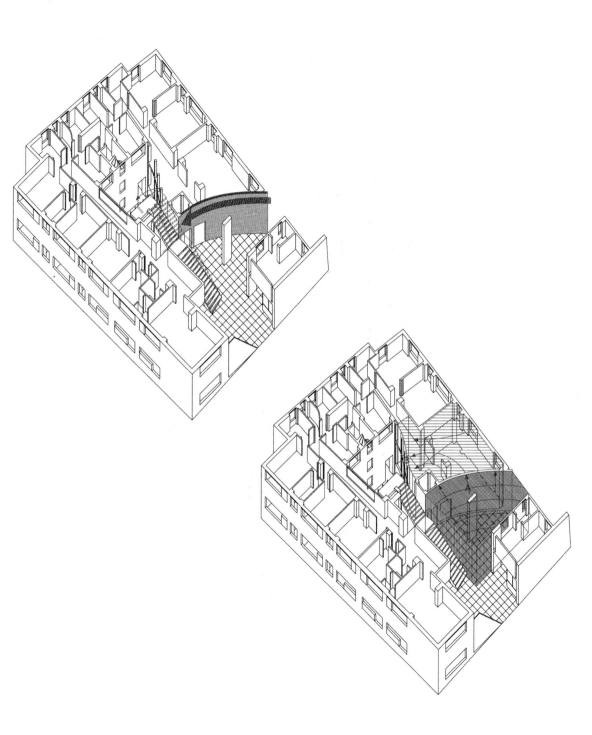

L. Moretti, Casa
del Girasole, Rome,
axonometric diagrams

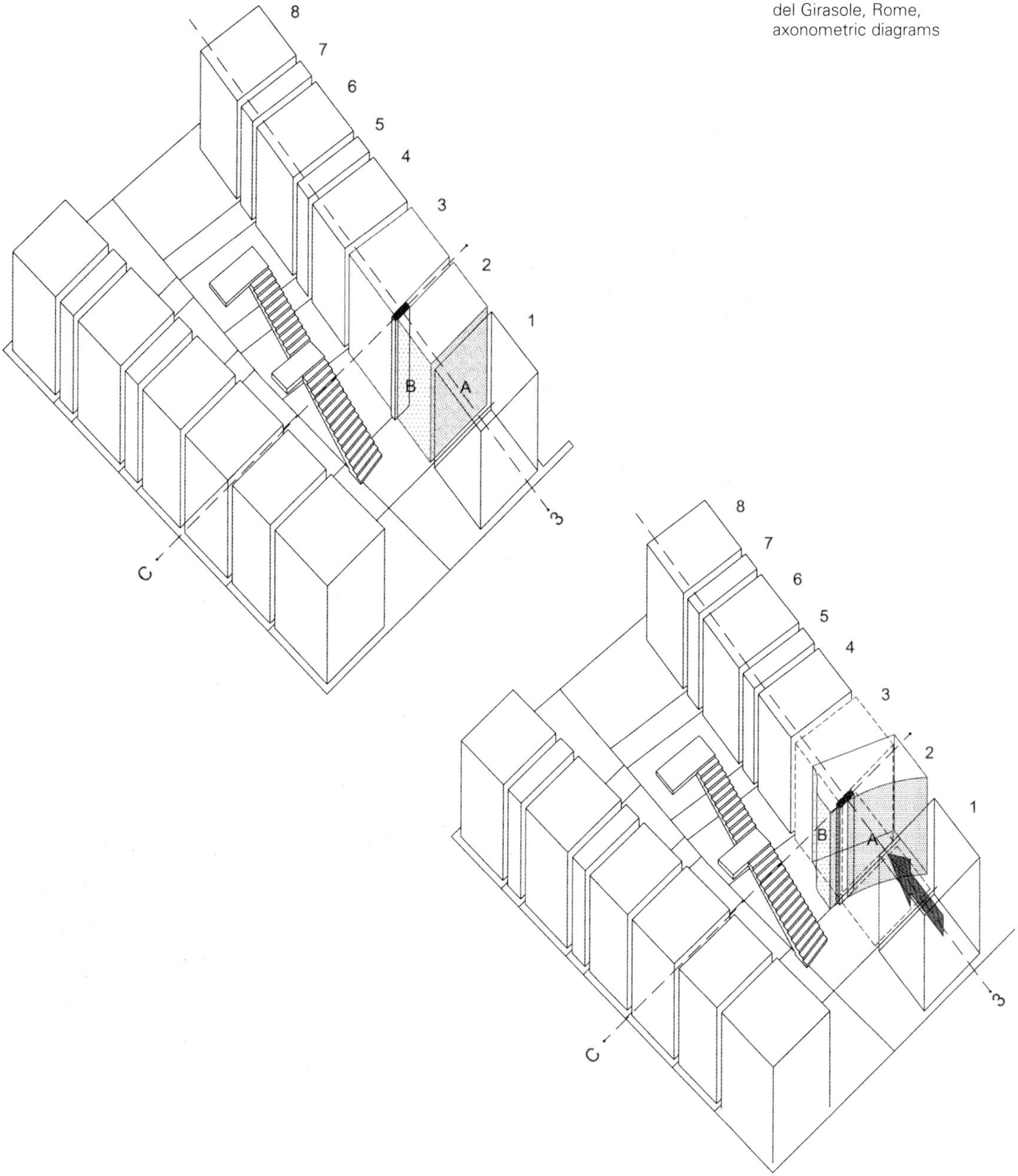

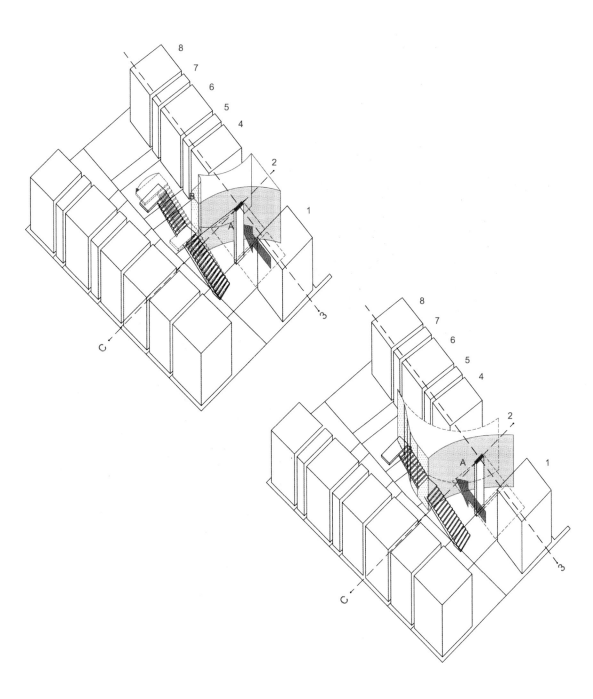

A Critical Analysis: Giuseppe Terragni

Giuseppe Terragni's Casa del Fascio and Casa Giuliani Frigerio can be called examples of critical architectural texts in that the meaning of their façades, plans, and sections can be read as displacements from an architecture of origin, hierarchy, unity, sequence, progression, and continuity to one of fragmentation, disjunction, contingency, alternation, slippage, and oscillation. In this sense the Casa del Fascio and the Casa Giuliani-Frigerio raise questions about their historical status as Fascist architecture, which is in part dependent on an identification, by some historians, with such criteria as classical ordination, monumentality, scale, and other rhetorical devices. The Casa Giuliani-Frigerio is an architecture that communicates ideas, but not primarily by the traditional method of elaborating a simple configuration into a more complex one, or by decorating an enclosure with architectural "warping and woofing". It is not an architecture that is the end product of a process that begins with a simple geometric object. Rather, the Casa Giuliani-Frigerio may be described as the "decomposition" of a hypothetically prior, more complex entity. Its unstable, asymmetric conditions testify to this: an element is registered in relation to a particular configuration in one view, only to be registered to a second and perhaps completely different configuration in another. When an observer attempts to coordinate the second reading with the first, the first falls away, and vice versa. This sets up a condition of oscillating readings as opposed to the alternating readings that were dominant in the Casa del Fascio. The difference between these two types of reading is crucial. In the Casa del Fascio, there are stable readings that alternate from one to the other. In the Casa Giuliani-Frigerio, the constant oscillation between readings never allows for stable readings to fully cohere.

The language of architecture has historically shifted from the culturally contingent to the conventional to the natural. When the language of architecture is understood as natural, the question of the possible is removed, and cultural shifts in architecture are limited. Formal displacements, articulations, and experimentation can be posited as critical in this regard, in that they do not assume that the condition of an architectural language is objectively given but rather that it constitutes a series of unarticulated repressions. Dominant among these is the idea of historical precedent and stable and transcendent origins. The formal can be critical precisely because it operates on the borders of historical precedent. While all architecture engages formal components, the formal is potentially critical when it participates in the invention—or reinvention—of disciplinary languages not simply for the sake of invention alone but as an analytical commentary on disciplinary precedents. While it cannot be said that all formal manipulations are critical, this argument thus raises the question of whether an architecture can be critical without formal manipulations.

In this sense, the two buildings by Terragni would seem to challenge Manfredo Tafuri's assertion that the idea of the critical is always embedded in the concept of history. Establishing an inherent connection between the critical and the historical assumes that architectural language is given or can be fully known a priori. In this context, the potential development of a critical notation as opposed to the gestural—its possibilities—is restricted, since such a view of the historical assumes that the realm of possible repressions is already known. The difference between Tafuri's idea of the critical and the idea of the critical proposed here hangs on this issue.

Can it be said that certain types of architecture are more open than others to complex textual readings? Is this quality inherent in the architecture or in the methodology of reading? Unquestionably any building can be read textually through a privileging of, for example, its functional, structural, social, and aesthetic codes. Thus it can be said that all architecture can be read textually. It can also be said that no architecture is more inherently textual than any other. But the thesis posited here is that certain conditions of architecture are particularly open to textual readings that displace canonical interpretations through the use of a primarily formal discourse, defined within the parameters of a historical period. That is, certain buildings loosen the relationships between historical, aesthetic, and functional conventions and in doing so encourage readings that not only entail the internal recognition of such shifts but also displace the conventional notions of reading. Such displacements are here called *critical*.

(Excerpted from P. Eisenman, "Terragni and the Idea of a Critical Text," in *Giuseppe Terragni: Transformations, Decompositions, Critiques*, Monacelli Press, 2003. First published in Italian in 1996).

G. Terragni,
Casa Giuliani Frigerio

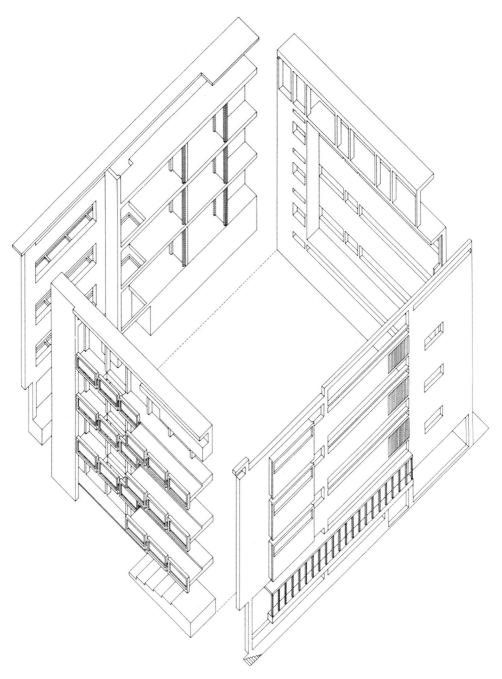

Casa Giuliani Frigerio,
south-west corner

Casa Giuliani Frigerio,
north-west corner

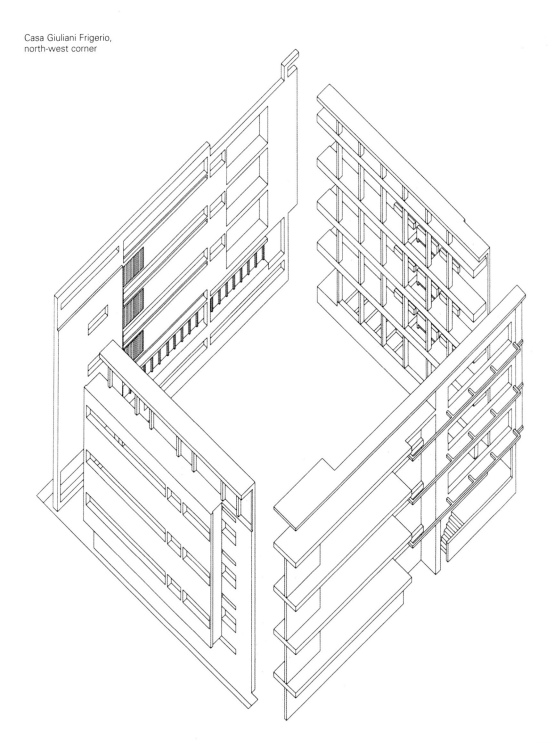

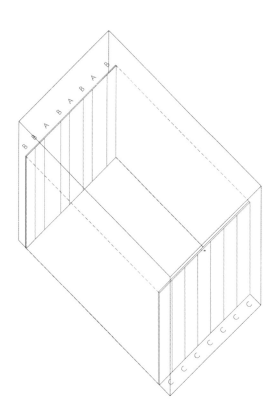

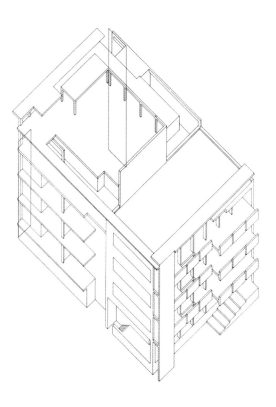

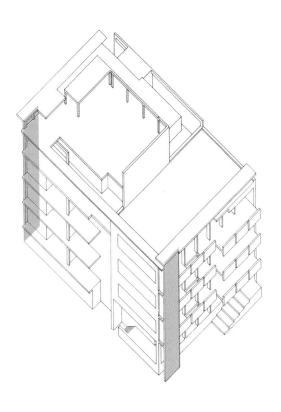

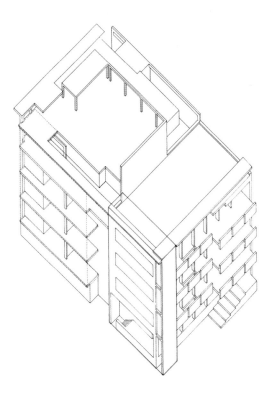

Project Research

House II
Hardwick, Vermont
1969-1970

House II is concerned with a systematic development of two ways in which information may be conceived of and derived from the interaction of formal relationships. To articulate these ways of conceiving and producing formal information in House II, certain formal means were chosen, each involving an overloading of the object with formal references.

This development can be seen first from a set of analytic diagrams. These diagrams describe the development of a set of abstract formal propositions as a possible condition of an underlying structure and their initial transformation into a specific environment.

Any given coordinates of space can be described as either linear, planar, or volumetric. The coordinates of a cubic space are described by its edge or its center: the edge composed of lines or planes, the center by a line or a volume. In this particular house, the center condition is arbitrarily defined by a square volume. From this, the original square is divided into nine squares. These squares are marked by a matrix of 16 square columns. The first six diagrams present one set of conditions possible from this initial definition. The selection of the conditions as opposed to any other condition of such a deep structure is, at this stage of work, arbitrary. Figure 2 shows the gridded nine-square arrangement. Figures 3, 4, and 5 select and isolate three possible conditions of that gridding: as a matrix of 16 columns, as a series of four planes, or as a series of three volumes seen as solids between the planes. It is to be noted that the planar and volumetric conditions are linear and directional in opposing axes. While there are obviously other combinations of planes

and volumes, these chosen oppositions suggest one prior condition of an underlying structure which when transformed will produce a level of implied or virtual information in the actual space. Thus while the grid of nine squares can be seen as an underlying structure, the axial opposition of planes and volumes can be seen to create a transformation of this structure. The assumption here is that these initial spatial oppositions in some way permit the articulation of a virtual relationship between the actual environment and underlying structure.

The further diagrams concern the development of one possible transformation from this underlying structure to an actual environment. A second transformation, following from the initial deployment of lines, planes, and volumes, was a dislocation in the form of a diagonal shift. (This can also be seen in the dotted outline of two bounding volumes in Figs. 2–6). This shift created the potential for developing another set of oppositions in the actual environment by articulating two squares, one defined by the planes and the second defined by the matrix of columns. The particular location of columns, walls, and volumes produced by the diagonal shift creates two datum references. It is possible to read the shear walls as a neutral referent, especially when seen from the north, whereupon the columns can be read as the residue of these planes, transposed diagonally from them (Fig. 9). Alternatively, the columns can be read as a neutral referent, especially when seen from the south, whereupon the shear walls may be read as having been shifted from the plane of the columns. The column grid also acts as a neutral referent for a second set of formal readings involving a diagonal cross-layering. One diagonal is articulated by the volumes of the upper level, which step up and back from left to right. This movement crosses at right angles the diagonal established by the shear walls (Fig. 10), which repeat and reduce in length as they move along the diagonal from the full-length shear wall at the north. Because of this diagonal shift, the implied planes formed by the columns and beams cut through the columns in such a way as to create a condition in space where the actual space can be read as layered. The layering produces an opposition between the actual geometry and an implied geometry; between real space, which is negative or void, and the implied volume, which is positive or solid (Figs. 11–15). This layering also produces a plaiding in both axes. Implied solid volumes can now be read on either side of the original column datum. The residual volumes are further articulated by the location of the roof skylights, which are placed directly over them in the north-south axis.

The particular way that the formal structure is developed through a diagonal shift manifested in a structural redundancy is perhaps only one means to make such formal concepts as compression, elongation, and frontality become operative. While the diagrams which attempt to describe these relationships are analytic, nevertheless they are potentially an integral art of the design process. In addition, the diagrams act as a set of instructions; they attempt to make legible the relationships that an individual may not see. They provide what can be called a conceptual framework for this understanding.

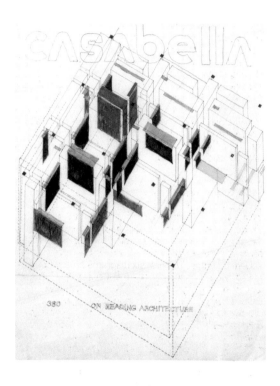

(Excerpted from P. Eisenman, "Cardboard Architecture: House II" in *Five Architects: Eisenman, Graves, Gwathmey, Hejduk, Meier*, New York, Oxford University Press, 1975).

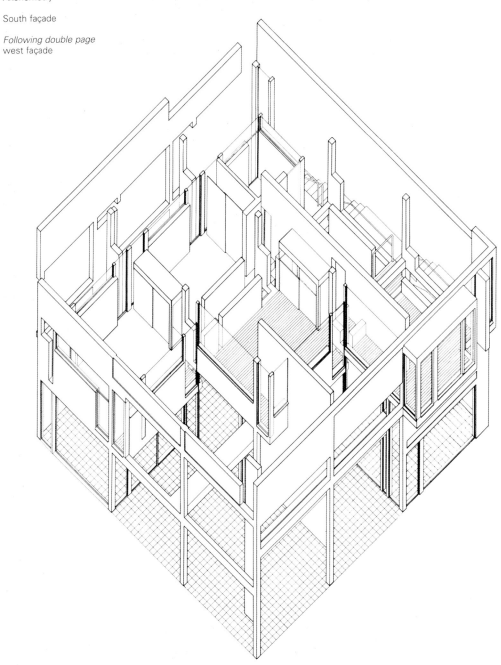

Analytic diagrams

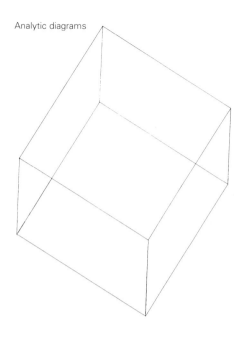

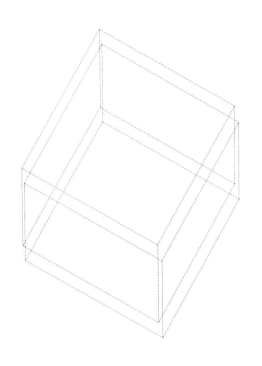

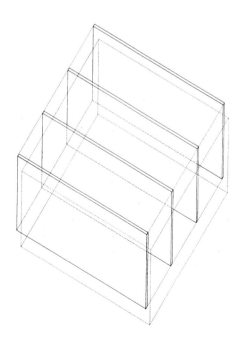

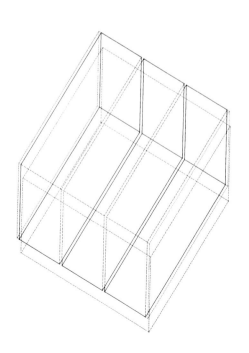

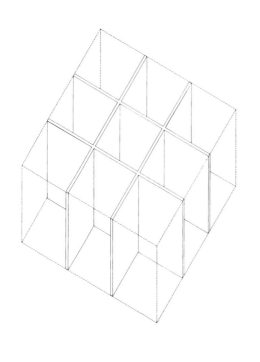

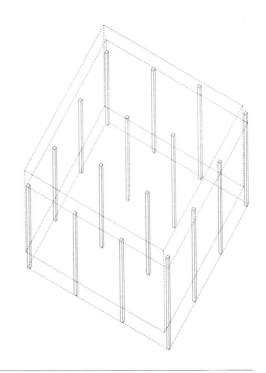

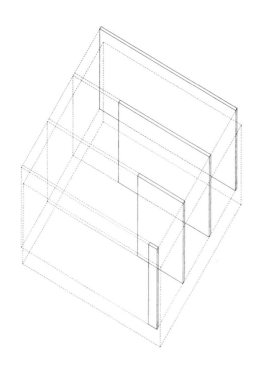

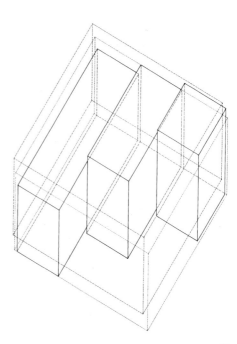

Analytic
diagrams

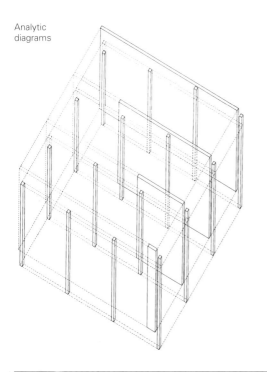

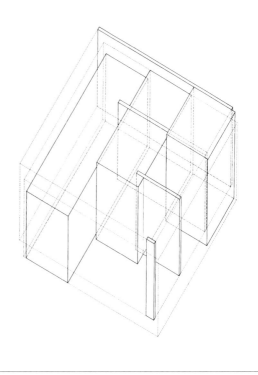

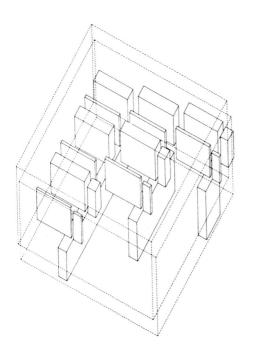

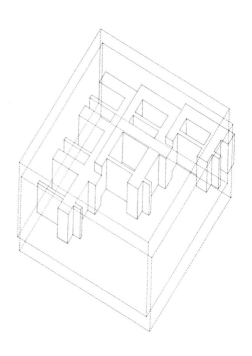

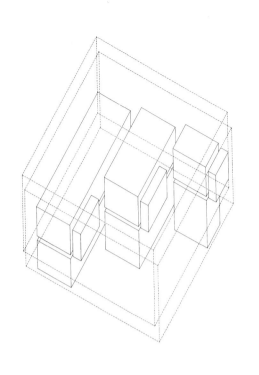

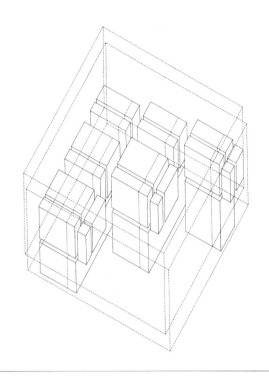

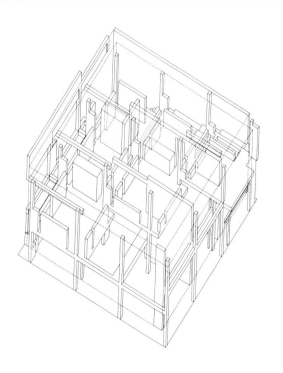

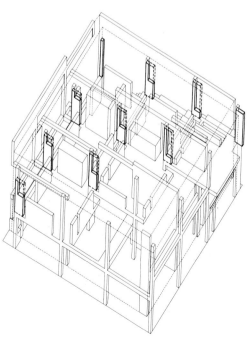

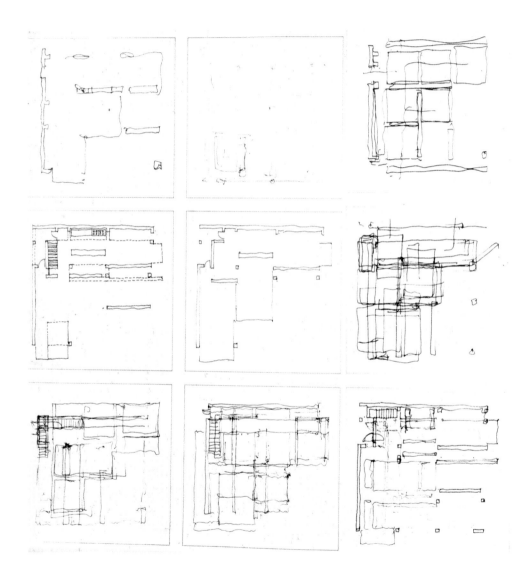

External detail

Following double page
external view

Cannaregio Town Square
Contest for the area of Cannaregio
Venice, Italy, 1978

In 1978 the Municipal Government of Venice held an invited international competition to design a major public open space in Venice. The project started from the notion of an architecture that invents its own site and program. Rather than trying to reproduce or simulate an existing Venice whose authenticity cannot be replicated, it constructs another, fictitious Venice. In this case, the gridded structure of Le Corbusier's Venice Hospital, designed in the 40's, was continued and used as a structure over the given site. This grid is marked as an absence, a series of voids, which act as metaphors for man's displacement from his position as the centered instrument of measure. In this project, architecture becomes the measure of itself.

The objects which inhabit this landscape are variations of an earlier project, House 11a, shown at different scales. The smallest object is too small to shelter, but raises the question whether it is a house or the model of a house. The middle-sized object may be a house, but it contains the smaller object inside. Is it a house, or a museum of houses? The largest object is twice the size of the middle-sized object. What can this object be called?

The sequence and the relationships between the objects are intended to place into question the idea of meaning as an effect of function. The fiction created acts as a notation and a critique of existing institutionalized definitions. The imaginary metaphysical landscape exists in contrast to the surrounding urban context, yet at the same time enhances its energy.

Text One: The Emptiness of the Future

The Cannaregio is the site of Le Corbusier's Venice Hospital project—one of the last anguishes of heroic modernism. The hospital program is symbolic of modernism's remedial ideology. Its complete grid is superimposed on the irregular context of Venice. Text one continues the imposition of Le Corbusier's grid on the entire Cannaregio. This grid is articulated as a series of voids—holes in the ground. These holes are potential sites for future houses or for future graves. They embody the emptiness of rationality.

Text Two: The Emptiness of the Present

The second text constructs several objects that appear to be part of the existing context—contextual objects. Upon close examination, these objects reveal that they contain nothing—they are solid, lifeless blocks which seem to have been formerly attached to the context. On the ground is the trace of their movement, their detachment from life. They leave a trace, mark the absence of their former presence; their presence is nothing but an absence.

Text two also constructs a second series of objects. These objects deny the existing context in order to establish the primacy of the context of the voids. While all the objects have the same form, the form of a house, they appear at three different scales. The first object is smaller than a house, the second is the size of a house, the third is larger than a house. The three different scales do not only change the way man possesses objects in terms of their physical presence but also in the way they are named. The first object is about five feet high. It is smaller than a man but usable to the extent that he can crouch in it and it provides shelter. So, is it a house or a model of a house? The second object is the size of a house, but inside it contains the shell of the first object and nothing else. The first object is a replica of the exterior of the second object. Is it a house, a tomb for itself, a model of itself, or a real object? If it is a mausoleum, then the first object, the five-foot "house," is no longer a model of something real but a reality itself, no longer a model of something else but so-mething in itself. The change of the name, from house to mausoleum, changes the reality of the first object from model to house. The third object is twice the size of the second object. Inside it contains the second object containing the first object and nothing else. How is it named? It is not the scale of a model, a house, or a mausoleum. Can it be a museum of houses or a museum of mausoleums? Which object is the house, if in fact one of them is a house; which one is the "correct" size; which one is the real object? Since both of the larger objects contain a smaller version of themselves, is the smallest object the real object and the larger objects merely containers for the smaller? The three objects together stand at the limits of architecture both in terms of their scale and their naming.

Text Three: The Emptiness of the Past

The third text constructs a diagonal line in the ground. This line is the topological axis of symmetry for the objects and a physical cut in the surface of the earth. The earth's surface is peeled back slightly, as if the skin of some unknown body, suggesting that there is another level, some "inside," which cannot forever be suppressed by or submerged under the rationality of an axis. It suggests something that may erupt and that perhaps will not stay down—the unconscious or the shadow of memory.

Giordano Bruno was an alchemist. He practiced the art of memory. He was brought to Venice in 1600 at the request of a rich nobleman, and there he was incarcerated and eventually burned at the stake for practicing his art. Alchemists thought that through mystical intervention they could turn dross into gold. The model of Cannaregio is painted gold. It is the gold of Venice and it symbolizes the mysticism of the alchemist. The objects are a pink-red. This is a Venetian red and it symbolizes the martyrdom of Bruno. The colors remind us of the irrationality of a Venice in 1600 turned against the art of memory. Today, seemingly "rational" projects for Venice have embraced memory. All three memories—future, present, past—have their shadows, the loss of memory. Perhaps we must now learn to forget.

(Written by P. Eisenman for the Cannaregio project *Three Texts for Venice*, 1980)

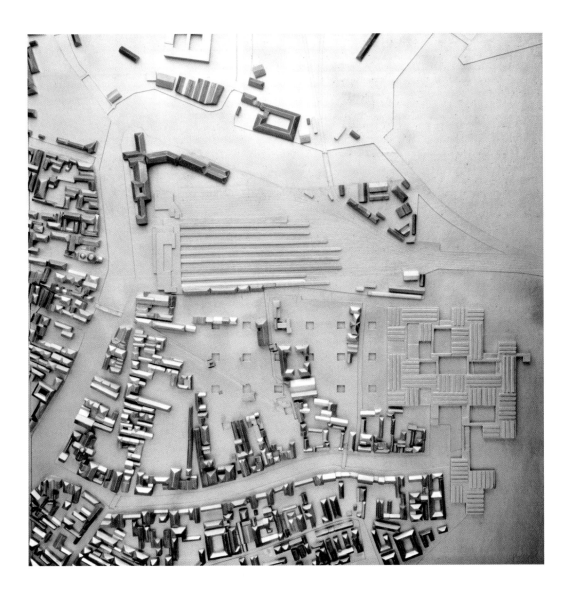

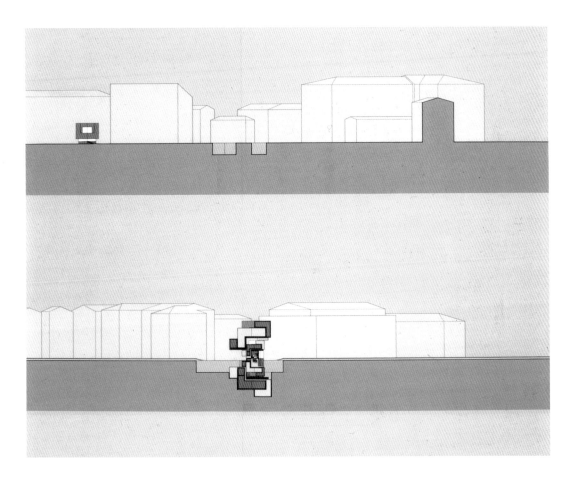

House X
Bloomfield Hills, Michigan
1975

House X is a point of departure from the earlier houses, for it has to do with a suspension of certainty—a
move away from rationalism and formalism as a justi-
fication for discourse and a strategy for design. Moreover, the house is not so much a new non-rational model as a search into the nature of other models in architecture, which may suggest an "other" relationship
of culture to the object.

There are three basic aspects of this change in attitude apparent in House X: the first concerns the nature of the design process in relation to the architectural object; the second concerns the nature of this object in relation to the architect and to man in general;
the third concerns the nature of object both as an object and as a sign.

The process in House X is no longer about the ma-
nipulation of what in the earlier houses was a preferred
set of linear and planar elements and a sequential, linear progression through a readily reconstructive series
of transformations, but rather is about a notion that is
called "decomposition". This term suggests an activity analogous to what literary critics call "deconstruction". Deconstruction is basically an analytical device;
here it does not suggest any particular attitude toward
either the process of making or toward the physicality
—the actual literary, or in this case, architectonic
essence—of the object produced. For this reason, and
also in order to avoid the term "construction", which
in architecture usually refers to the process of building
and fabrication, the word "decomposition" is used because the concern here is more with the process of design and composition.

Decomposition searches for unknown orders and
origins that do not develop through transformation. The
result of decomposition is a simulation that can be verified only when it is achieved. Thus, random selection
is not the appropriate beginning of decomposition. Instead, an act of approximation—the notion of a starting point as a heuristic device—that suggested itself as
a beginning for House X – a process in which at each

stage sets of alternative configurations suggested themselves and implied either a consistency or correspondence (that the configuration followed logically from
and suggested the one before it) or an inconsistency
and lack of correspondence (that the configuration did
not follow logically from and did not suggest the one
before it).

Through a dual process of selection after successive stages of approximation, an object began to evolve
whose configuration suggested the potential nature of
such a process. The process, then, became one of dis-
covery, in which the goal was the revelation of formal
consistencies or regularities often through inconsis-
tencies or incongruities, perhaps suggesting pre-exis-
tent concepts or new ways of grouping elements, but
in which the beginning and end point remained undefined and the chief principle was uncertainty: a working forward in time and backward in space.

The specific configurations of House X can be understood initially as the juxtaposition of four squares.
This configuration is only an initial analogue, a heuristic device used to approach a more complex sign condition, which in itself will be only a possible approximation of the reality it signifies. And in fact, the final
configuration will be seen as a cumulative attempt to
dissolve its own seeming connection with any initial analogue—in other words, the final plan will be only a series of traces which refer in a sense forward to a more
complex and incomplete structure rather than backward to a unitary, simple, and stable structure. It thus
becomes a kind of pre-distillation of this more complex "future" condition. This process continues from
the larger scale of the whole to the smaller scale of the
parts, until there is some point of exhaustion at the
level of the smallest objects.

(Excerpted from P. Eisenman, "Transformations, Decompositions, and Critiques: House X", in *House X*, Rizzoli International, New York, 1982.)

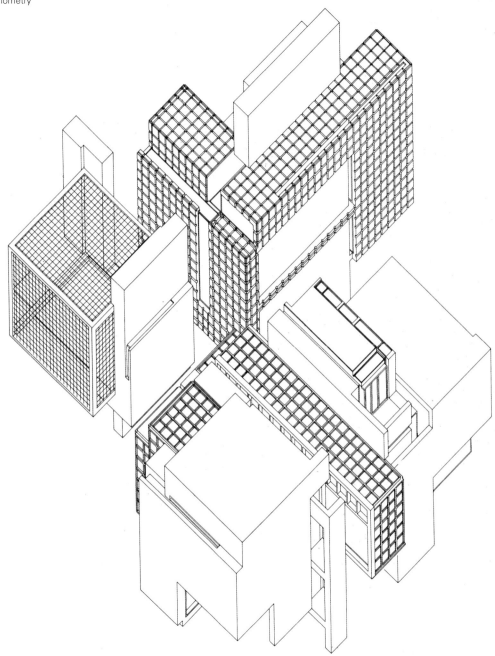

Collage of the west
and east façades

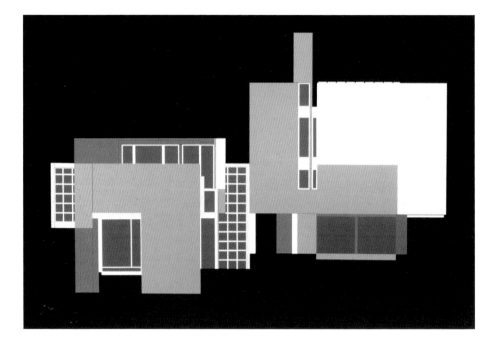

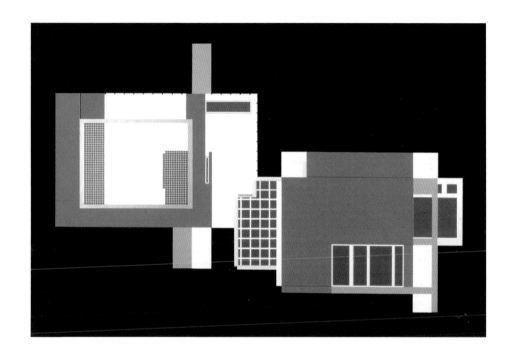

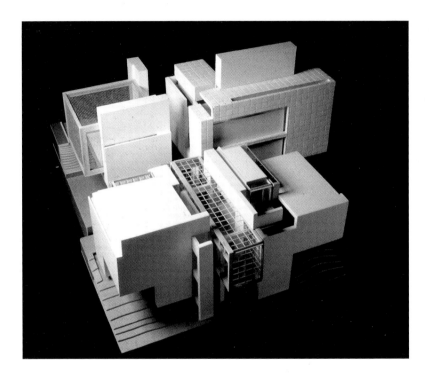

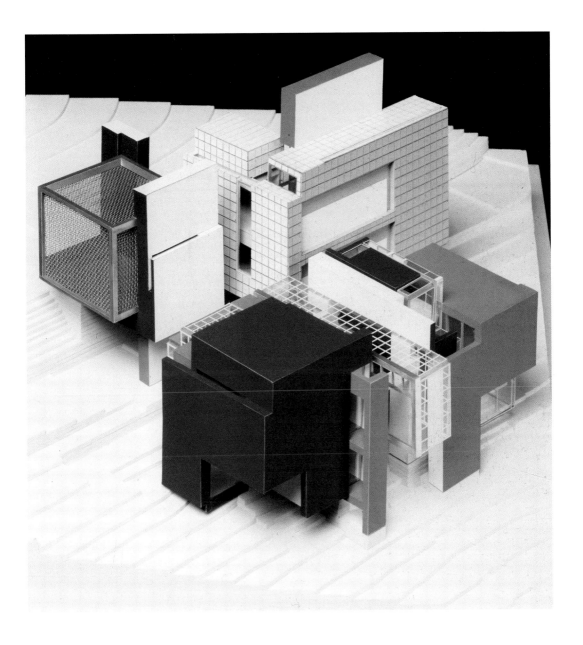

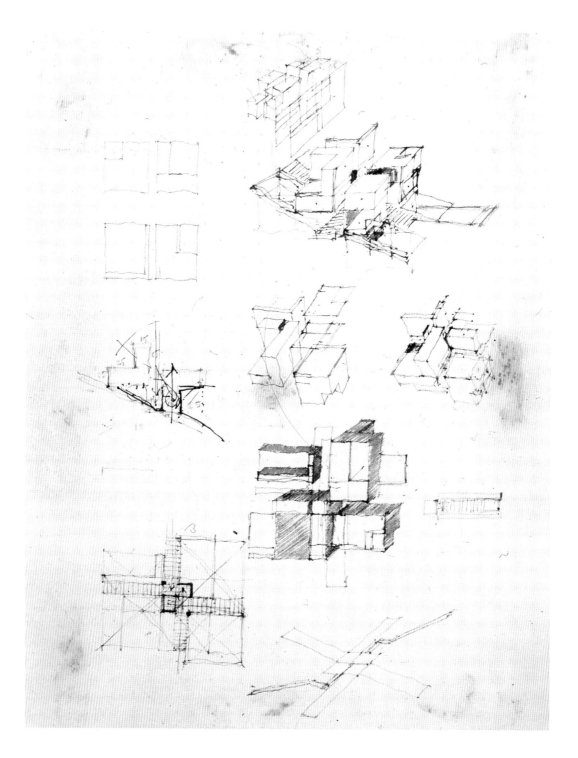

Beyond the Diagram.
Iconography, Discipline, Architecture
Pier Vittorio Aureli, Gabriele Mastrigli

"It appeared to me more fitting to follow up the real truth of a matter than the imagination of it."
Niccolò Machiavelli, *The Prince*.

1. Post-modern

The post-modern, contrary to what Lyotard maintained, is anything but the end of the great narrations. Indeed if it is viewed from a broader historical perspective the post-modern reveals itself as an impressive narration, greater and more robust than that which it overcame, in other words the modern.

In architecture post-modernism was enclosed within a shorter phase when compared to the period that philosophy and culture in general has identified as being the post-modern age; it identifies a style in relation to the past, a reaction therefore only when compared to another style: modernism. In this manner architecture has exorcised the post-modern to the point of removing it. Recent history has taught us, on the other hand, that post-modern culture cannot be reduced to a style, a book, a Venice Biennial, or a critique of the Athens Charter; rather, the premature viewing of a phenomenon in a historical perspective so as to overcome it immediately, and thus consume it as has been done periodically over the last thirty years, constitutes the very logic of post-modernism, whose peremptory stagnation is nurtured precisely by post-modernism's ability to identify with the very principle of change. Postmodernism, emended by the moral imperative of development, coherently with a modern attitude, has inherited the obligation to overcome as a repetition compulsion, without any connection to objectives or intentions other than change itself. It is the principle of *change*, therefore, that is the core of post-modernism, a stable principle that reflects what we could call a structural condition of western culture since the ancient Greeks, whereby all things are thought as temporal, contingent and transitory; contemporary thought has brought this condition to its extreme consequences over the last two centuries declaring the death of all absolute truths that claim to resist the test of time.

In this sense the dawn of post-modernism could be set at the turning point between the end of the eighteenth century and the beginning of the nineteenth century, when the French Revolution decreed the fall of the absolutist state and liberated the *individual* for once and for all, an autonomous subject at the mercy of the future, who together with liberty also won the right/duty to testify to the crisis of every eternal and

P. Eisenman,
House X, sketches

111

unchangeable truth. This crisis was to be expressed in its most radical form by Nietzsche in the idea of the "death of God", that is to say the destruction of that unquestionable knowledge (*epistéme*) which from Plato to Hegel had formed the very sense of western thinking.

Faced with the collapse of the immutable, art and architecture looked to history, which, being the extraordinary invention through which Renaissance man ordered time (as he controlled space through perspective), offered itself at this point as the last, desperate attempt to oppose the future building ever more absolute structures against it. By identifying its own rational laws and establishing its own philosophy—aesthetics— art and architecture called for their own autonomy. An autonomy which unfolded itself through the neoclassical and established a radical return to its origins, but not seen as an unlikely exodus towards the past, rather to hypothesise the most definitive future possible: a future where art, modelling an "absolute" past, implied less and less a concept of the world and ever more a concept of itself. This process rejects every feature of "genius" and transforms itself into method and therefore, into pure *technology*.

It is no chance that all the nineteenth century neo-historicist revivals following the neoclassical period up until Art-Nouveau, despite appearances, established the pre-eminence of technology over history. A pre-eminence—but we could also say a changing of the guard—which marked the principal route towards the advent of modernism and consecrated technology as the very heart beat of change.

For this reason postmodernism must be viewed today as something that went far beyond a mere return to the stylistic features of the past during the eighties and was consumed and forgotten within a decade. It appears instead to be a cultural device that has accompanied the progressive destruction of the foundations, the principles and values of western thinking over the past two centuries[1]. Having withdrawn faith in the foundations, the world appears, says Nietzsche, like "a work of art that gives birth to itself", a world where art is the wish for power in its pure state, a clear form where technique incarnates things to come, precisely because it is obliged to recognise the ontological necessity of what is *new* while it subtracts any value from it.

This ontological necessity of what is new, deprived of any objective— or this faith in the future as a conviction that things unquestionably come out of nothing and return to nothingness—is exactly the same attitude that science permitted at the beginning of the nineteenth century with the advent of electromagnetism. Indeed the discoveries of Volta first and then Maxwell concretised the idea of the flow of electric current, the invisible energy of the "new" modern society, generated for the first time in a stable and continuous form. From this moment on human existence is guided by numerous, invisible energy systems through which science and technology celebrate things to come. It is through the production and control of such things that the transformation—and therefore the very meaning—of the world is enacted and definitively removed from the creative hands of any God.

Within the sphere of the future, once the baton has been passed from History to Technology, architecture began to fine-tune the devices used to control the transformations of the world. At the end of a long neo-historicist period, the modern movement, in the words of Le Corbusier, explicitly declared: "The truth lies in the diagrams!"[2], in other words it is not conceivable to control the transformations of the world without precisely representing the "new" forces in play. If already by the end of the forties architecture, and especially urban planning, put through the works by science, entrusted its destiny to the diagram as its privileged analytical device, both in interpreting the past as well as hypothesising the future—think on the one hand of the geometric schemes whereby Wittkower analysed Renaissance architecture and on the other the functionalist coeval bubble diagrams used by Gropius in Harvard –, it is with the neo-avant-garde of the sixties—a forerunner of the digital era—that the diagram in architecture abandoned the traditional representative guise and began to take on the appearance of a real *deus ex machina* of the future, precisely that "abstract machine" which, according to the celebrated definition of Deleuze and Guattari, "does not function to represent, even something real, but rather constructs a realness that has yet to come, a new type of reality"[3].

The diagram is, therefore, the new device through which the post-modern stance clearly shows its *nihilistic* dimension, not only in architecture, systematically imposing new realities that transform and therefore substitute previous ones, in other words the fidelistic conviction that things can be created from nothing and can be returned to the nothingness from whence they came. This is a dimension that contemporary culture has exalted and implicitly adopted as positive to the point of making it the fundamental trend of our times[4].

2. Modern

The representation of what we define as *contemporary* is developed through a temporal pattern that grows more and more complex, dense with changes, so dense that change itself actually becomes one immense state of *fluctuating stagnation*.

Architecture in this stagnation has been represented for some time now in ten-year periods, in decades, the measure in which the inexorable and ever accelerating cycle of history is constructed.

Periodization in decades is a recent practice in historiography. It seems to have started in the forties of the last century when it was used to identify the thirties as a strongly characterised, cultural block, distinguishable, on first inspection, from the preceding period. Such recognition marked an acceleration in the succession of movements and styles imposed by a "fashion system" that was always more integrated within the media machine.

It is unrealistic today to criticise this system, as it is to exalt it as a means of development in so much as it *exists* and is deeply rooted in the generative processes of culture on a par with style, language and taste. Actually fashion (*moda* in Italian) could coincide with *modern* as it shares the same etymological root. Indeed the adjective *modernus*, which appears in the Latin language from the fifth century[5], it was used to distinguish between the recent Christian world and the ancient world. *Modernus*, therefore, indicated *recent* and therefore *new* and, as such, was considered to be a restrictive term as it was used to signify something of lesser duration when compared to what went before, in other words antiquity. But within the meaning that it has acquired historically, "modern" is quite different from "moda" (fashion) in so much as the former in its classical connotation coincides with history, understood as a gradual process of accumulation, while the latter corresponds to the "the imposing character of novelty: what is in fashion meets consensus through the mere fact that it is the most recent thing, consequently all the rest is *"antiquated"*[6]. In this sense, if fashion (like style) is now *naturally* accepted, what is modern (like what is classic) is not accepted at all. It is a *choice* that involves taking a dialectic stance and, therefore, a critical *continuity* with those things, which, as such, are liable to opposition and accumulation.

Simplifying, we could state that modern is a constituting fact, while fashion is a transitory fact. The double register put forward in the celebrated historiographical definition proposed by Giedion is useful so as to take on a non-hysteric attitude towards that which appears as *novum*, as critics often do, always equally divided between enthusiasts and sceptics. Instead it is necessary to be able to pinpoint the possible *constituting facts* in the *novum*, especially when that *novum* becomes a victim of itself, in other words when it is not yet history but something *just past*, the recent past, "yesterday's news".

3. Constituting Facts

Allen Ginsberg, introducing *Desire*, Bob Dylan's masterpiece recorded in 1975, stated that "every generation-decade flowers in the middle" and, recalling the events that had left their mark on American culture over the previous decades—*Poetry Reinassance*, the beginning of the Berkley protests against the Vietnam war—he hinted at the fact that Dylan's record would become a *constituting fact* of the seventies, taking its place within the continuity of history of which it *consciously* intended to be the peak in that moment. Also within the development of Architecture the half way years of a decade have given rise to what was the constituting fact of that decade. Starting from the outset of periodization in decades, from 1925, the year Le Corbusier's Esprit Nouveau Pavilion was built, to 1955, the year of the *Home for the Future* of the Smithsons and 1966, when *Complexity and contradiction in architecture* by Robert Venturi was published as well as *L'architettura della città* by Aldo Rossi, or 1975 the year of the Frank House by Peter Eisenman and finally 1995—just ten years ago—, when *S,M,L,XL* by Rem Koolhaas was published, the last great *constituting fact* of architectural culture, the paradigmatic value of which has yet to be surpassed. Despite the numerous clones that have been created from this last fact—first and foremost those by Koolhaas himself—and despite the fact that the book itself has broken with the ranks of architecture once and for all, often with problematic results, the book itself remains one of the most absolute "perfect acts of architecture". In this sense S,M,L,XL stands in *continuity* with other "perfect acts" such as—to stay within the limits of the postmodern odyssey—the forty-year studies on Terragni by Eisenman, the equally-long studies on the American city by Venturi and Scott-Brown, those by Léon Krier on the urban planning of European cities, studied that do not seek the development of contemporary culture in each presumed phase but rather set down some generalised features, starting, paradoxically, from unique, radical, personal or controversial hypotheses. These examples, even before generalising, stand out in virtue of their uniqueness, their own architecture, their unequivocal choices, formulated however as an attempt to take a continuous critical stance on what has been achieved and perceived before also disclaiming it. In this sense the fundamental characteristic of these *perfect acts* lies precisely in their *hieratic character*, in the sense that Le Corbusier gave to this term: "the condition in which a civilisation finds itself when, leaving behind an empirical period, it becomes aware of something which previously had only been sensed"[7]. Hieratic character is opposed to the dictating character of the new because, contrary to the intermittent nature of the latter, the former is first and foremost "*self-awareness*, the final moment of a long period of research which is reached through acquired consciousness"[8].

Contrary to this, the first half of this confused and traumatic opening decade of the new century seems to be characterised by several declarations of intent: ranging from ever more all-inclusive (however vacuous) research programmes to moralistic returns to the order of the profession, premature historicization and enthusiastic transport towards a radiant future.

In this climate dominated by theoretic babble or fatalistic consent, two "new" paradigmatic horizons appear to be trying to impose themselves as constituting facts, attempting to overcome the interdisciplinary urban "realism" which in various forms has pervaded and characterised the nineties: on the one hand is a renewed (almost fetishist) interest in *iconography*, which proposes to distil the most picturesque aspects of that realism, rendering it comprehensible to the public at large and still exploitable on communication channels; on the other hand is a explicit return to the substance of the *discipline* understood not as architecture but rather as the profession or better still the *machining of production*[9]. This return to a sort of metaphysics of the profession is an attempt to redefine the very operative structure within which architecture can and must act, a clear sign of how lies, which are notoriously short-lived, did not allow the interdisciplinary euphoria of the nineties, fed by the flash fire of the *new economy*, to overcome the serious political, economic and cultural crisis of the millennium.

4. Iconography versus Discipline

If there is something pathological in the architecture of the past forty years, something that is evident in all its problematic nature, it is certainly the iconographic character many architectonic events. Despite the fact that architecture and urban planning over the past fifty years has been pervaded by the ambition to render *reality as found*, reality has had right of access in architecture only in the form of *icons* images and signs. If modern architecture is founded on an epistemology of experience, on an effective participation in reality, post-modern architecture, with its iconographic superabundance, seems to have identified completely with the spectatorial epistemology of consensus. To meet the taste of the latter architecture has tried to be *plausible*.

In the beginning this plausibility was established through the formal attributes of architecture, whereby an asymmetrical façade or one with an advertising sign was already seen as *complex and contradictory*. Subsequently this plausibility was brought about through programmatic contents, whereby an innocent shopping mall was categorically transformed into a *generic space*. Finally today plausibility in architecture is expressed through sophisticated and widespread *merchandising* which attempts to acquire consensus by naively replicating the *empire of signs* of which we are inexorably prisoners[10].

Erwin Panofsky distinguished between what he called *iconology*, meaning a method of interpretation based on the exertion of synthesis, from what is commonly called iconography, in other words that which is "simply a means of proceeding that is purely descriptive"[11]. The iconographic efforts of much architecture in relation to the world, despite ambitions of symbolism and content, is nothing more than tautological descriptive gesticulation before complexity; a procedure which demonstrates, as Pasolini would have said, an extreme refusal of the interpretative responsibility that form inevitably demands even in the most compromised situations thus falling back on a symbolic, generic, abstract, vague and redundant plausibility, in many ways incomprehensible and consequently grotesquely superfluous. It is enough to think of what Charles Jencks defined as "a new paradigm"[12], in other words *iconic* architecture, which is, in reality, nothing other than a monumental and improbable *melange* of exercises in high-tech, a condensation of arbitrary symbolisms, self-celebratory engineering feats imposed by a public ever more instantly dazzled by spectacle and always more indifferent to the actual experience of the world.

In opposition to the iconographic tendency in architecture from Venturi to the more recent Koolhaas it would appear that today there is a certain *rappel a l'orde*, an ill-concealed nostalgia for discipline, understood as professionalism and craftsmanship, which arose even before disciplinary nomadism failed to produce the results that were naively hoped for. This presumed professional rigour founded for the most part on the deterministic materialism of digital technology is, on a par with plausible realism, another "metaphysical branch" which tries to eliminate the real and effective circumstances that condition architecture. In reality this *return* to order is not towards architecture, yet again it keeps its distance, but towards the professional discipline itself, like a normative coagulation which defines the new paradigms of architectonic *production*. If in the nineties architecture, particularly so-called digital architecture, was enchanted by the myth of interdisciplinarity and dispersion into other disciplines, today some of its major exponents moralise about a new disciplinary chastity, investing new technologies with the task of announcing the latest "Copernican" revolution: if the forms produced by mechanical technology were fixed, stable and solid, the forms produced today, thanks to electronic technology, "change and are in endless transformation"[13]. As a single algorithm can generate an infinity of mathematical functions, and consequently different forms, such a *possibility* would be the very essence of architecture, the ultimate scope of which would be summed up in the laughable "moral duty to exploit all the potential of present-day technology", producing an infinite sequence of unique pieces[14], therefore the destruction of identity, the constituting and *necessary* trait of the so-called *non-standard* paradigm[15]. This destruction sanctions the triumph of technology over the discipline itself as it hypostasises a normative system with the objective of systematically bypassing the regulations. On the contrary the non-standard paradigm, in a desperate attempt to interpret the novel aspects of the times, ends up deposing contingent reality entirely because it shifts the axis of production into the deterministic world of infinitesimal calculus where, at its limit, it does not yield the object of observation, since "in non-standard production what counts is not the form of the product of the series but the difference between the products of the series"[16].

During the first digital period architecture invested in virtuality, flexibility, lightness and the ephemeral understood as essential elements of the contemporary landscape. Today this same culture has shifted towards a technocratic materialism that is as deterministic as it is exasperatingly complex which is not only symptomatic of a consolatory and weak-willed return (given the premises) to craftsmanship but also and especially of a profound uncertainty regarding the final objective of our work: architecture and the city, the reality of which, despite everything, continues to be part of our experience. All the above proceeds while the so-called non-standard architects of a burnt out and conservative *neo-avant-garde*, who dominate the scene today, concentrate all the more on spectacular monolithic objects the meaning of which, apart from filling the belly of a consensus which grasps only the most conservative aspects of these architects' projects, does not go beyond a narcissistic and superfluous self-celebration. Paradoxically those who until a short time ago sustained the pre-eminence of technical effectiveness of a product over the effective form, that is to say the performative "Young Turks" of the nineties [17], have given in to what they though to have buried with the production of myriad of diagrams, that is, again the *empire of signs*, the most trivially obvious analogy, the most rhetorically banal iconography, the most sentimental and populist symbolism.

Finally it is worth remembering that to define architecture as a professional discipline is tautological reasoning which, in the professional environment in which we operate, would mean reducing architecture to a legal definition: one belongs to the discipline when one pays one's taxes. On the other hand, in courageously defending the autonomy of ones own intelligence one cannot avoid coming to compromise with reality, starting from what is effectively and empirically arguable, the effectiveness of which leads to the premises for a return to architecture.

5. Diagram

A return to architecture is possible only by facing the fundamental misunderstanding through which post-modern culture has survived so long. This misunderstanding is what we could call the "metaphysics" of the diagram. From a simple representative convention and *white writing*[18] of architectural phenomena, the diagram is actually understood today in the fields of architecture and urban planning as a irreplaceable, irreducible instrument through which it is possible to reduce or increase all the complexities or contradictions in the name of a freedom justified by the ever more sophisticated means of production. In short, the diagram is seen as being the essence of the facts, their very "possibility" to quote a celebrated passage from Gilles Deleuze's book on the pictorial language of Francis Bacon[19].

If the diagram in the iconographic approach is still the instrument for interpreting the future, firstly representing its transformations and then, with growing insistence, reconstructing its transformation to the point of becoming a substitute of architecture, the disciplinary prospective, in its attempt to restore an operative role to architecture, leads the diagram back to the "abstract machine" hypothesised by Deleuze which "never functions in the direction of representing a pre-existing world, but produces a new species of reality, a new model of truth"[20].

But this new reality produced by the diagram is never seen as a stable reality; it is programmatically transitory, changing, elusive and fragmented into infinitesimal portions of time, "a flow—says Sanford Kwinter quoting Bergson—that inflects, combines and separates and leaves nothing not transformed"[21]. The objective of the diagram, its "truth" is, therefore, the necessary, incessant creation/destruction of reality, a desire for power or dominion over the forces that tear things from nothing and return them again to nothingness.

It is not by chance that the advent of the diagram in architecture coincided, after the second World War, with a period of maximum faith in science and engineering in particular as applied to military industry, when technology perfected its devices of systematic and *definitive* implementation of the principle of change: controlled nuclear processes, the management of radar signals, prototypes of territorial information networks, ballistics, cryptography; a principle by which the implementation of the new and its recognition *coherently* implies its destruction and therefore the cancellation of all of its possible value. It creates no scandal moreover that today, at the height of our technological civilisation, the diagram stands, in the words of its latest apologists, as nothing other than "the motor of novelty, whether good or bad"[22].

For this reason the diagram—within the meaning given to it by the greater part of contemporary architecture—fails both as a new iconography of reality (because it wishes to represent not reality but production and therefore, creation from nothing), and as the new motor of production (because it postulates necessary and *immediate* destruction). What it gives us, therefore, is a prospect without hope, without a future but at the same time—which is much more serious—it is extraordinarily unaware of the destiny that is in store for us; a destiny which, on the contrary indeed, is exorcised through the rituals of a deceptive and optimistic virtuality the representation of which is a conjuring trick where the devastating consequences of this nihilistic attitude are replaced by an arbitrary and reassuring concept of the future.

From this point of view we would be tempted to say that the diagram in architecture is the real "essence of nihilism"[23], the means through which every "new" theory can create its own representations of the world *from nothing* and drive it back to nothingness. But it is precisely for this reason that the diagram, far from being the "rise of another world" sanctions the *impossibility* of any world because it always wants and only wants to be the "possibility of a fact" and never "the fact itself"[24], the liturgy of the cult of the future which demands the sacrifice of every necessary connection between things, every bond, every causality and consequently the definitive and inexorable *cancellation* of things themselves.

This cancellation, far from being perceived in its actual dimension, is, instead, the simplistic device by which every theory today can start from scratch. Indeed both the iconographic tendency of architecture and even more so the disciplinary tendency, underline their compliance today to the "metaphysics" of the future, establishing their pertinence to the world on *nothing* (after all was *Imagining Nothingness* not the great post-modern manifesto of the eighties and nineties from which all the present transitory facts are derived?).

In the ever more metaphorical and unrealistic implications of the diagram, as it is put forward by the iconographic and disciplinary points of view, lies the maximum unawareness of architecture when facing its own destiny. In front of this cul-de-sac which involves a much vaster and more important environment than architecture itself, it—even within the history of the western world, which is itself the history of nihilism—still has the opportunity to look at its own work and return to considering the sense of *being*. "Because—Severino states—this is where the most important task lies: to truly think of the impossibility that being cannot be, and to understand being no longer as a pure indefinite or a limited dimension, but rather as the concrete whole of things and events"[25].

6. Architecture

The position expressed in these considerations must be related to the reality of planning which in itself constitutes faith in the future. Architecture is always and in any case construction and therefore transformation (and therefore destruction). An awareness of the nihilistic background in which all western thought inevitably develops does not exempt architecture from carrying out its mandate which is to reform and transform the idea of city without taking refuge in its own false awareness of discipline, but also without celebrating every possible, superfluous representation of the world.

This position implies a condition for the theory of architecture: that it cannot abandon the future of the world without ever *selecting, constituting and institutionalising* such facts as would produce consequences on the experience itself. This implies firstly an emancipation form those forms of *discourse* which are nothing other than cannibalism of the same discourse, in other words gratuitous self-consumption in the name of an evolution whose only objective lies in discursive practice itself. The dynamics of ongoing change instead must be founded on the awareness of the inexorable stability of the constituting facts of architecture as forms. Through these constituting facts it is possible to reconstruct the concrete material on which to "consciously" found the issue of change understood not as rhetorical abstraction, in other words the *diagram*, but rather what Niccolò Machiavelli defined as "the real truth of a matter"[26]. This real truth should be understood here as architecture itself, its form, its syntax placed each time in the fullness of its concrete and current dimension of which architecture itself fixes the principles, tackling and solving this dimension from the inseparable relationship between being architecture and the future.

It is through the assertion of this effective dimension of the architectonic object that it is possible to avoid the unconscious annihilation which is recognised as being the fundamental tendency of our age; a tendency that has inevitably enveloped all the ideologies that have followed one upon the other in ever accelerating rapidity over the past fifty years—organicism, neo-rationalism, disciplinary autonomy, radicalism, pragmatism, urban realism, digitalism and finally the jaded return to discipline of our times opposed to the gesturing iconic trend.

Contrary to these ideologies, which in final analysis are no more than the coded messages of a community which is always more isolated and self-celebrating, the actual recognition of constituting facts—those we have called *perfect acts of architecture*—develops a critical continuity which permits the overcoming the very logic of post-modernism which has always stressed the more ideological and discursive aspects of these facts, consuming, often arbitrarily, the casual context that produced them.

It is precisely the rereading of these perfect acts of architecture, apart from their function as diagrams of ongoing change, that we are freed from their looming presence as yet unsurpassed texts by the exasperated theoretical industry of our age, now populated only by "philosophers without works".

The constituting facts of post-modernism appear to trace two routes. The first is one which we could define as the "song of 'genius', in other words the power with which the 'genius' sings the vacuity of everything"[27], in a certain sense the role that figures such as Koolhaas and Eisenman have taken on in bringing the post-modern "oppositional" attitude to extreme and dramatic consequences within a "sublime" project deliberately without hope but with extreme lucidity.

The second route, though more difficult, seems more decisive for the next generations and has already been taken by Le Corbusier, and comes from the consideration that it is not possible to decide to quit the history of the western world. Therefore, paradoxically, it is precisely this keeping with the western world that leads to a different way of operating (including architecture) within it.

This way of operating will have to deliberately and ruthlessly consider the nature of creating architecture and architecture itself as an object, but not to reach the umpteenth useless "death of architecture" or hermeneutic paranoia that has plagued architectural thinking in these last burnt-out years of "discourse about discourse", rather it should approach the architectural project with acute awareness of its task, of the problems to be solved, of its own singularity, the irreducible dimensions of which nurture the generalising character of architecture as a universal human phenomenon.

The generalising character, which an architectural work can potentially nurture, cannot be founded on generic iconographies or disciplinary expertise, which are nothing except mere *ideology* and in no way *theory*, but must be founded precisely on the awareness of the absoluteness of the architectonic object. Architecture is not the arbitrary diagram of everything, but the *idea* of an *everything*, starting from its consistency as a tangible form-object, or rather its actual existence within the history of the western world. In this sense architecture, *precisely because it is part of the future of the city*, reminds us of the nihilistic spectre inherent in the idea of the future, a spectre that looms over our experience of things and that we celebrate exasperatedly denying the very substance of the world.

But "when, beyond nihilism, every work appears diseased, operating so that this is evident is already *something different* than operating in a way that ignores its own disease. The works too then are different; also the acts of everyday life. Also the building of a house and of a city shows its non-truth, but carrying within itself the alienation and extreme violence of nihilism, it also brings with it, and in a way manages to show, a refusal of alienation and violence"[28].

This refusal is anything but a generic disassociation from the contemporary world. Instead it demonstrates the intention to not give in definitively to that falsehood which pervades all our actions and words, and it is already a positive thing per se because it lets us see the concrete existence of things, their peculiar understanding, their fortuitousness, their unavoidable appearance in our world, while it refuses the vague, abstract generalisation within abstract categories such as those that have been created thanks to the pervasiveness of the diagram as a reassuring surrogate for the reality of the world. Refusing devious conformism, implicit in many present-day diagrams, and returning to the awareness of architecture as a form-object means returning precisely to what Le Corbusier defined as the *hieratic character*, or rather that which distinguishes a modern work and understands it, not as the latest means of imposing what is new, but as a deep definitive, inexorable *awareness of one's self*.

[1] It is no mere chance that the new language of a tolerant and pluralist post-modern architecture was "founded" by Charles Jencks on the ruins of the Pruitt-Igoe apartment blocks in St. Louis, which "happily" announced the "death of modern architecture". Cf. Ch. Jencks, *The language of post-modern architecture*, Rizzoli, New York, 1977, p. 9.

[2] "Truth from diagrams" is the title of a chapter of *La Ville Radieuse*, where the exact, diagrammatic organisation of human life is the fundamental prerequisite "to place a 'theory' back in its true frame" according to Le Corbusier.

[3] G. Deleuze, F. Guattari, *A Thousand Plateaus: Capitalism and Schizophrenia*, Castelvecchi, Rome, 1996.

[4] The points put forward in this paragraph can be read further in the works of Emanuele Severino, in particular *La tendenza fondamentale del nostro tempo*, Adelphi, Milan 1988 and (edited by Renato Rizzi), *Tecnica e architettura*, Raffaello Cortina, Milan, 2003.

[5] For a history of the term "modern" see: H.R. Jauss, *Literary History as a Provocation to Literary Theory*, Bollati Boringhieri, Turin, 1999.

[6] G. Chiurazzi, *Il Postmoderno*, Bruno Mondadori, Milan, 2002.

[7] Le Corbusier, *On Modern Painting*, Christian Marinotti, Milan, 2004, p. 210.

[8] *Ibid.*, p. 211.

[9] *Machining of production* was the definition of the architectural discipline given by Alejandro Zaera-Polo during a public debate with Peter Eisenman held at the Berlage Institute in Rotterdam in the autumn of 2002. The transcript of the conversation under the emblematic title of "Return" will be published on *Hunch*, n. 9, *Disciplines*.

[10] The recent considerations of Rem Koolhaas are valid for all these cases: "Liberated from the obligation to construct, [architecture] can become a way of thinking about anything—a discipline that represents relationships, proportions, connections, effects, the diagram of everything", in AMO/OMA, Rem Koolhaas, &&&, *Content*, Taschen, Cologne, 2004, p. 20.

[11] E. Panofsky, *Meaning in the visual arts*, Einaudi, Turin, 1999, p. 36.

[12] "Several key buildings show the promise of this transformation—those by Americans Frank Gehry, Peter Eisen-

man, and Daniel Libeskind. There is also a vast amount of other works on the edge of the new paradigm by the Dutch architects Rem Koolhaas, Ben van Berkel, and MVRDV; or the Europeans Santiago Calatrava and Coop Himmelblau; or those who have moved on from high-tech in England, such as Norman Foster. These architects, as well as those that filtered with Deconstruction—Hadid, Moss, and Morphosis—look set to take on the philosophy." Ch. Jenks, 'The New Paradigm in Architecture', in *Hunch, The Berlage Report* n. 6-7, 2003.

[13] M. Carpo, "Pattern Recognition", in *Metamorph. Focus*, catalogue of the 9th Architecture Biennial of Venice, Marsilio, Venice 2003, p. 45.

[14] *Ibid.*, p. 48.

[15] In reference to the exhibition *Architectures non standard*, Paris, Centre Pompidou, 10 December 2003 – 1 March 2004, where the following groups exhibited: R&Sie, dECOi Architects, Objectile, Asymptote, Servo, KOL/MAC Studio, Kovac Architecture, Greg Lynn FORM, DR_D, NOX, Oosterhuis.nl, UN studio. Catalogue edited by F. Migayrou and Z. Mennan, Paris 2003.

[16] M. Carpo, *Pattern…*, cit., p. 46.

[17] The so-called *Post-critical* generation widely represented during the last two Venice Biennials and all the major media events of the last few years. This generation made its debut on the international scene precisely half way through the nineties just after the deconstructivist generation. The conference "Anyhow" held in Rotterdam in 1997 marked their rise in the name of what John Rajchman then called "a new pragmatism". Included in their number were: Greg Lynn, Alejandro Zaera-Polo, Ben van Berkel and Sanford Kwinter in the guise of theoretic mentor. Finally the competition for Ground Zero saw the "Young Turks" returning to what not even their 'formalist' predecessors would have dared to propose: a spectacular, monumental and symbolic form. Cfr. C. Davidson (ed.), *Anyhow*, Monacelli Press, New York, 1997; M. Agnoletto, *Groundzero.exe. Costruire il vuoto*, Edizioni Kappa, Rome 2004.

[18] This is the sense under which some diagrams should be understood, for example some used by Peter Eisenman in his studies of the architecture of

Giuseppe Terragni. This type of diagram belongs to the idea of a form of writing that does not reduce architecture to *nothing*, rather it reduces it to *zero degrees*. Cf.: P. Eisenman, *Giuseppe Terragni, Transformations, Decompositions, Critiques*, Quodlibet, Macerata, 2004. Cf. R. Barthes, *Writing, degree zero*, Einaudi, Turin, 1972.

[19] G. Deleuze, *Francis Bacon, The Logic of Sensation*, Quodlibet, Macerata, 1999, p. 168.

[20] Id., *Foucault*, Cronopio, Naples, 2002. p. 54. Also in the epigraph of the text by Robert E. Somol, *The Diagrams of Matter*, in "ANY" n. 23, 1998, p. 23.

[21] S. Kwinter, 'The genealogy of models. The Hammer and the Song', in *ANY*, n. 23, 1998, p. 60. Italian translation in http://www.parametro.it/estratto252-253-it8.htm.

[22] *Ibid.*, p. 57.

[23] Cf. E. Severino, *Essenza del nichilismo*, Adelphi, Milan, 1982.

[24] G. Deleuze, *Francis Bacon...*, cit. p. 175.

[25] E. Severino, *Essenza...*, Adelphi, Milan, 1982, p. 136.

[26] N. Machiavelli, *Il principe*, in *Tutte le Opere*, Sansoni, Florence, p. 280. On these concepts see especially L. Althusser, *Machiavelli e noi*, Manifesto Libri, Rome, 1999, p. 20.

[27] Cf. E. Severino, *Tecnica e architettura*, Raffaello Cortina, Milan, 2003, p. 121.

[28] *Ibid.*, p. 102.

Guardiola House
Cadiz, Spain

An idea of place, or topos, has always been central to man's relationship to his environment. This design for a house researches the meaning of place, and how it has been affected by a changing understanding of the world. Since the time of the Romans, when the crossing of the cardo and the decumanus marked the topos of the Roman encampment, man has been defining place as the mark—whether a cross or a square, a clearing in the forest or a bridge over a river—of his struggle to overcome nature. Today two things have happened to bring the traditional forms of place-making into question. First, technology has overwhelmed nature—the automobile and the airplane, with their potential for unlimited accessibility, have made the rational grids and radial patterns of the nineteenth century obsolete; second, modern thought has found "unreasonableness" within traditional reason, and logic has been seen to contain the illogical. These challenges to order had been repressed by traditional reason, but in man's new condition, these ideas can no longer be repressed. In architecture this is seen in the questioning of whether man's marking of his conquest of nature is still significant, and further, in the acknowledgement that place (topos) has always contained "no place" (utopia). With this breakdown of the traditional forms of place has come a concurrent breakdown of the traditional categories of figure/ground and frame/object.

Since classical times there has been an other definition of place which suggested such a simultaneity of two traditionally contradictory states. This is found in Plato's *Timaeus* in the definition of the receptacle (chora) as something between place and object, between container and contained. For Plato, the receptacle is like the sand on the beach: it is not an object or a place, but merely the record of the movement of water, which leaves traces of high tide lines and scores imprint—erosions—with each successive wave receding to the water. Much as the foot leaves its imprint in the sand as the sand remains as a trace on the foot, each of these residues and actions are outside of any rational or natural order; they are both and neither.

This house can be seen then, as the manifestation of a receptacle where the traces of logic and irrationality are intrinsic components of the object/place. It exists between the natural and the rational, between logic and chaos; the arabesque. It breaks the notion of figure/frame, because it is figure and frame simultaneously. Its tangential L-shapes penetrate three planes, always interweaving. These fluctuating readings resonate in the material of this house, which, unlike a traditional structure of outside and inside, neither contains nor is contained. It is as if it were constructed of a substance which constantly changes shape—formed by imprints left in which mark an other position of the structure, before the interweaving. Then, the imprinted forms, which record movements of the pattern, are no longer either frame or object. Finally, the pattern appears again in the surface of two of the quadrants in the form of glazed and unglazed tiles, and the remaining quadrants are treated with a coral and white stucco surface to reiterate the duality of the reading. The house is neither an expressionist work nor one of mechanical precision. It rather has the qualities of a controlled accident, of a line, once put down, which cannot be erased, but in whose linearity is the density of unpredictable reverberations.

Progressive Architecture, Architectural Design Citation, 1989.

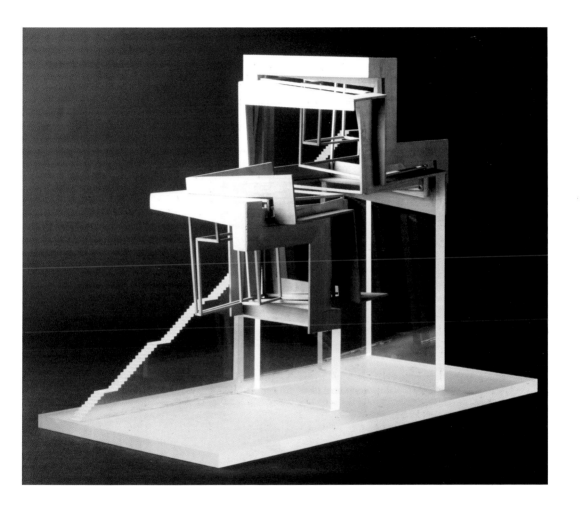

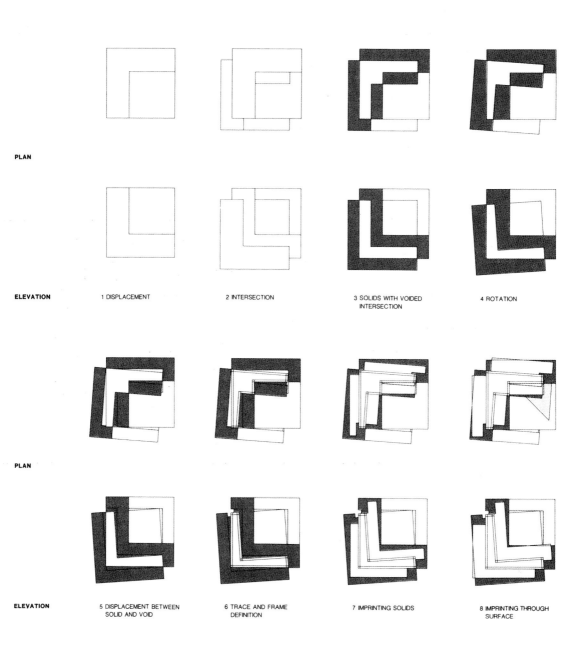

PLAN

ELEVATION

1 DISPLACEMENT

2 INTERSECTION

3 SOLIDS WITH VOIDED INTERSECTION

4 ROTATION

PLAN

ELEVATION

5 DISPLACEMENT BETWEEN SOLID AND VOID

6 TRACE AND FRAME DEFINITION

7 IMPRINTING SOLIDS

8 IMPRINTING THROUGH SURFACE

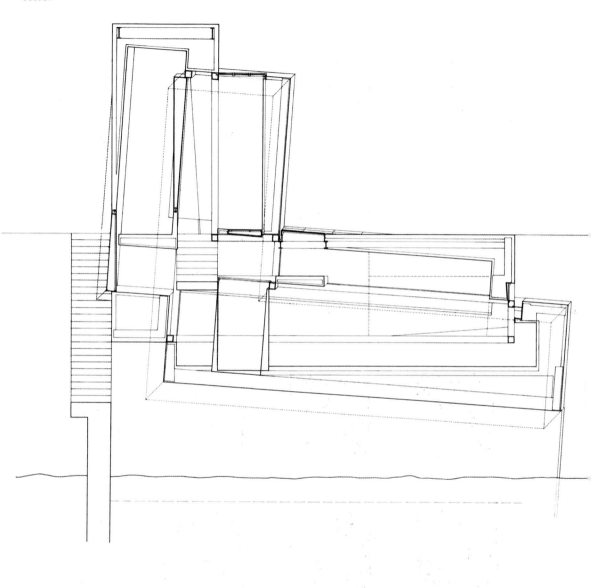

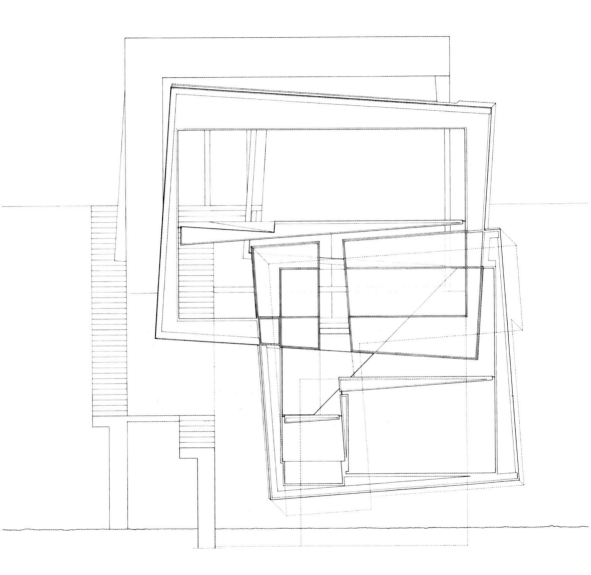

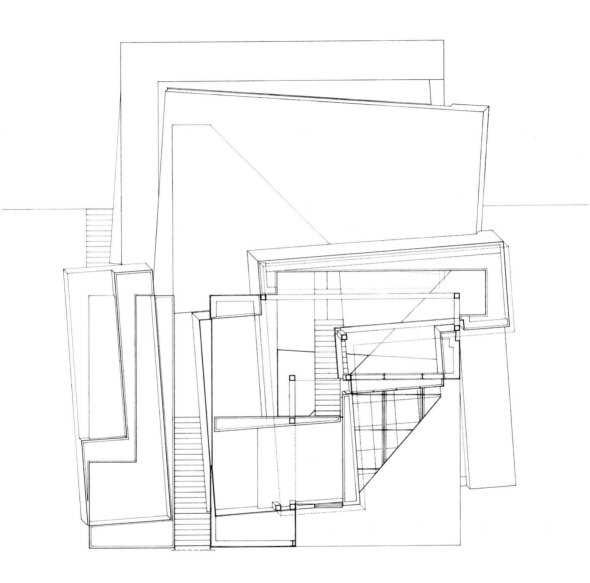

View of the plastic model
from south-east

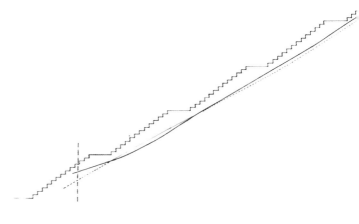

Section on the ground seen
from the east

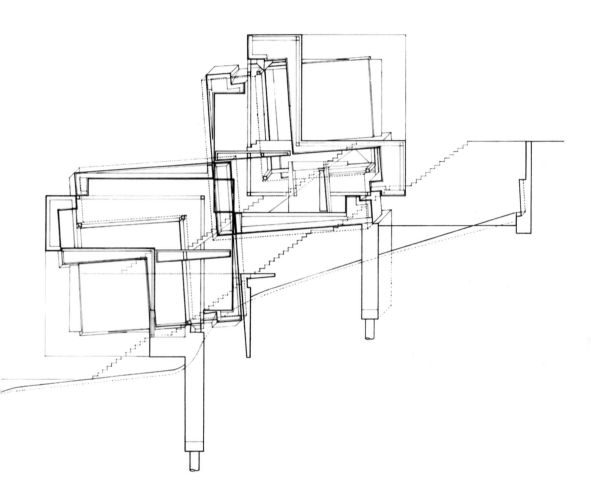

Structural model seen from the west

Structural model seen from the east

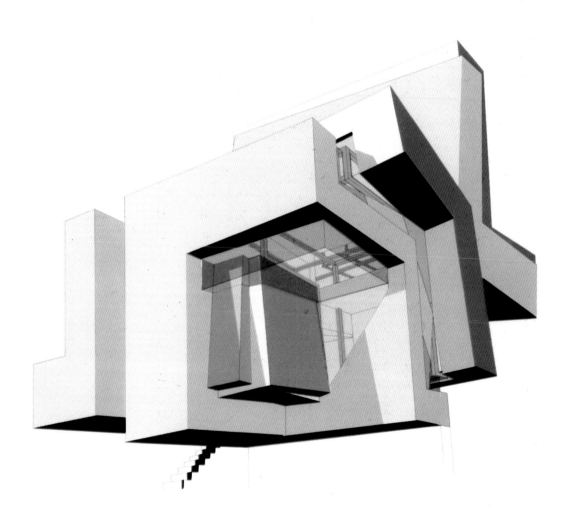

FSM East River Competition
New York, 2001

Eisenman Architects' two towers for a new mixed-use neighborhood of nine high rises located just to the south of the United Nations are vertical extensions of the topological matrix. The 80- and 60-story towers were developed through a process of making that attempts to invert the traditional tower formulation of base, shaft, and capital to give each building a new and unique identity.

Typically, the tower as a building type has had a tripartite formula associated with the classical column and its base (or lobby and street façade), shaft (repetition of floors) and top (or crown, like the Chrysler or Empire State buildings). The Eisenman towers for FSM are unique in the middle.

The FSM site is along the west bank of the East River, which, at the United Nations site, flows between the New York boroughs of Manhattan and Queens. The geography of these two island boroughs causes the city grid to shift; that is, the Queens grid does not align with the Manhattan grid. Using this shift in the urban grid to inform the making of the FSM towers, we placed the Cartesian square of the Manhattan grid at the virtual base of one tower and the Cartesian square of the Queens grid at the virtual top. These two squares were then extruded toward each other to meet vertically in space. This action produced a torqued, vertical shaft. The element of time was then added in the form of a compressive force, which acts on the top and bottom to produce the effect of a molten liquid flow at the middle of the tower. This flow approximates and images a nature of time.

The base and top of the new towers are Cartesian, while the "shaft" that connects them suggests a new nature, one that marks the flow of time over its surface. The process also produced unique residential floor plates throughout each tower and the possibility of duplex units at the midpoint of the towers.

Plastic model, view to the south

134

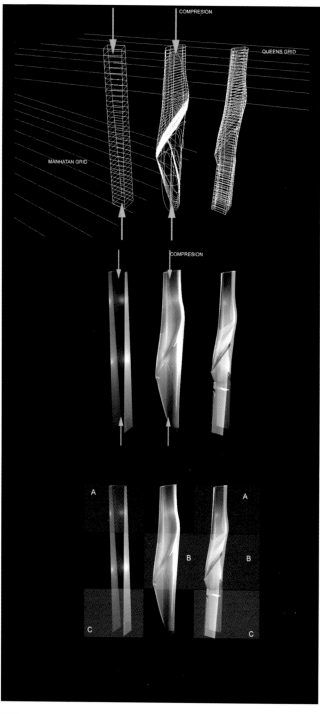

Diagrams of conceptual torsion

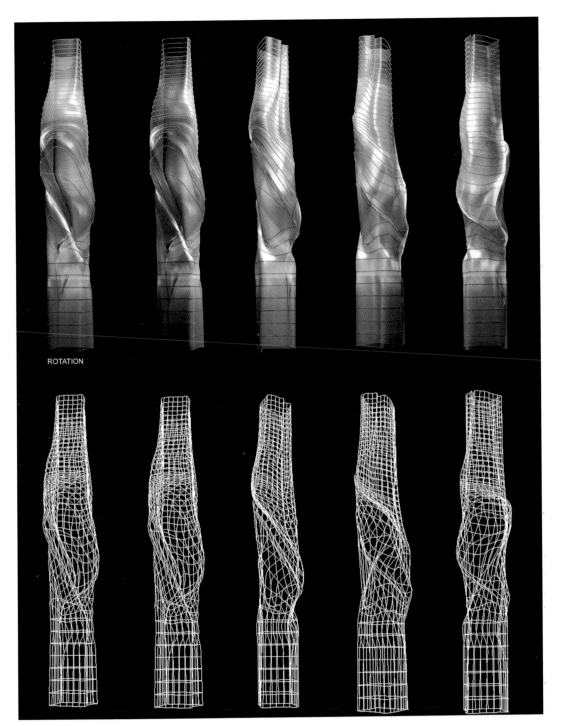

ROTATION

137

Plastic model

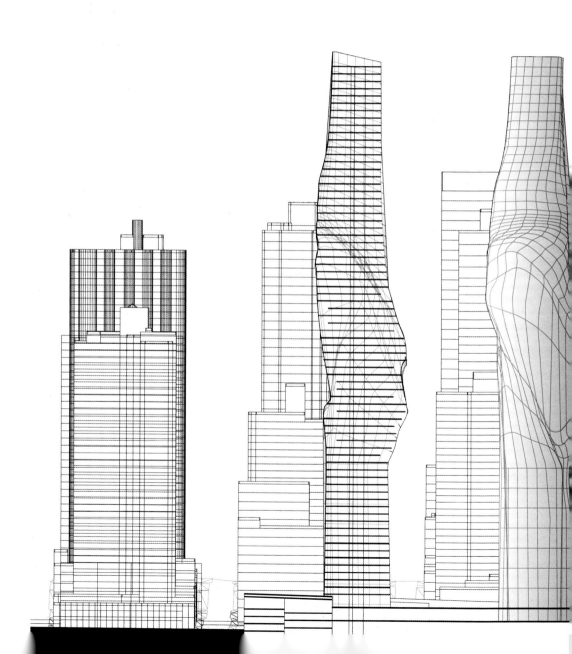

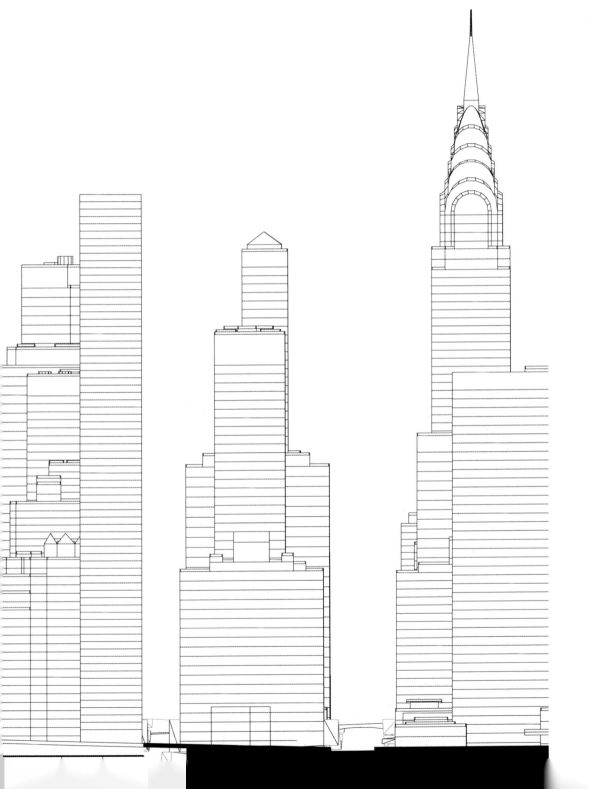

Photomontage

The Virtual House
Siteless Ideas Competition
1996

"The virtual is opposed not to the real but to the actual. The virtual is fully real insofar as it is virtual."
G. Deleuze, *Difference and Repetition*

In an abstraction of the existing spatial concept of House IV, two cubes are posed side by side to form a field for potential interconnectivity, upon which an abstract machine initiates a differentiating process. This spatio-temporal process of transformation leads to the actualization of the virtual through time and opens architecture to its own indeterminacy. Form is then reread as a manifestation of becoming, rather than a representation of function and meaning. The process of becoming changes the object in space and time, breaking any direct correspondence between real elements and their representation.

The program for the Virtual House begins from the memory of the spatial concept of Peter Eisenman's House IV, for which he wrote an unpublished text in 1987 titled "The Virtual House". Here the Virtual House is abstracted into cubes that constitute a potential field of internal relations and conditions of interconnectivity. Each potential connection can be expressed as a vector. Each vector has a field of influence that actualizes its virtual movement through time. This actualization is visualized through the effect of each vector on the lines within its field of influence. The lines and their geometric properties become forces. For each vector, attributes were set arbitrarily in order to describe its field of influence. The movements and interrelations were produced by these attributes, which are now seen as constraints that influence the loca-

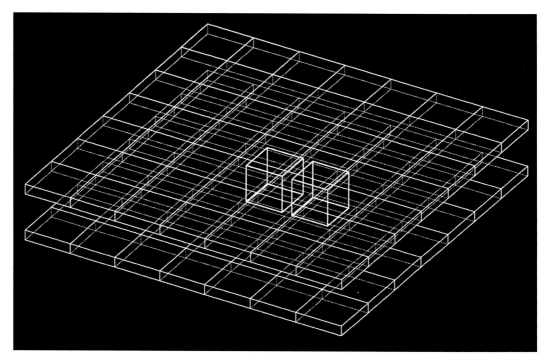

tion, orientation, direction, and repetition of any vector within the space. These constraints operate on each other as local forces. Each constraint acts and reacts according to three types of fields of influence—points, orientation, and direction. The condition of each vector is recorded, whether unconstrained or constrained, as a series of traces.

Deleuze writes in *Difference and Repetition*, "For a potential virtual object to be actualized is to create divergent lines which correspond to—without resembling—a virtual multiplicity". In the Virtual House, the virtual multiplicity is the changing memory of the two cubes, changes due to differences in their interrelations in time.

In addition to rethinking form, in this process the virtual characteristics of simultaneous activating and manifesting point toward an understanding of multiplicity and establish "real" distinctions between the given parts of a whole. One can no longer reduce complexity to simplicity. Contrary to the Cartesian notion of completion, the idea of incompletion is now operative. The continuous desire to realize the virtual generates new possibilities and alludes to another understanding of interrelations and repetitions.

Using the notion of the virtual in making architecture runs the risk of simply and literally materializing the immaterial. Hence one needs to address the productive making of architecture, that is, the condition of the virtual, in order to allow architecture to question traditional judgment. This allows for another working of space that affects both subject and object as architecture continues to become.

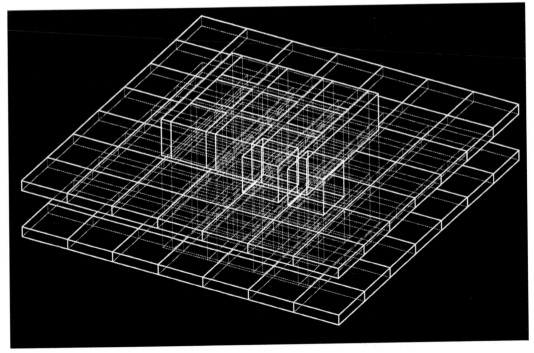

Conceptual diagram   "Butterfly"
of development

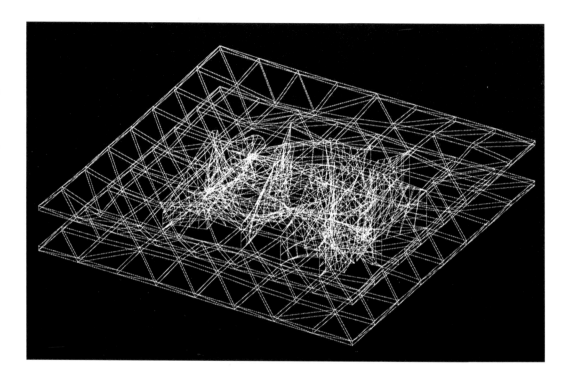

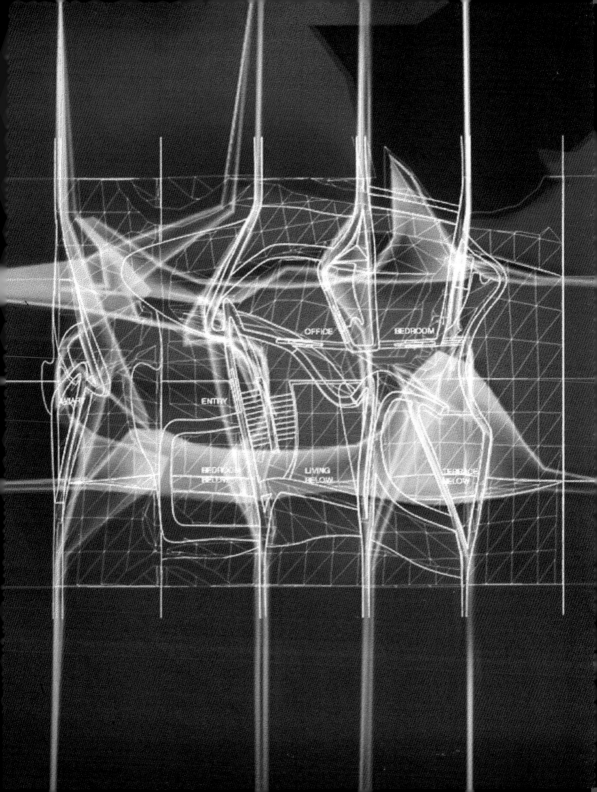

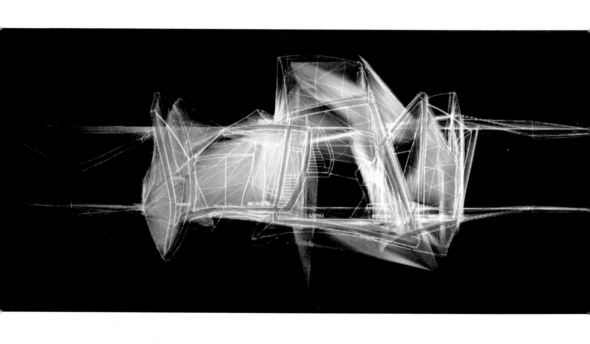

Plastic model

Following pages
Plan

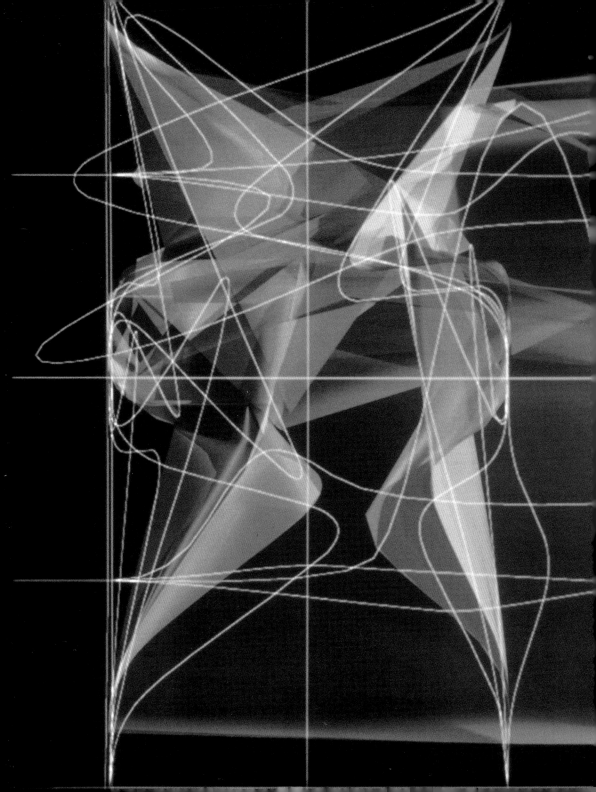

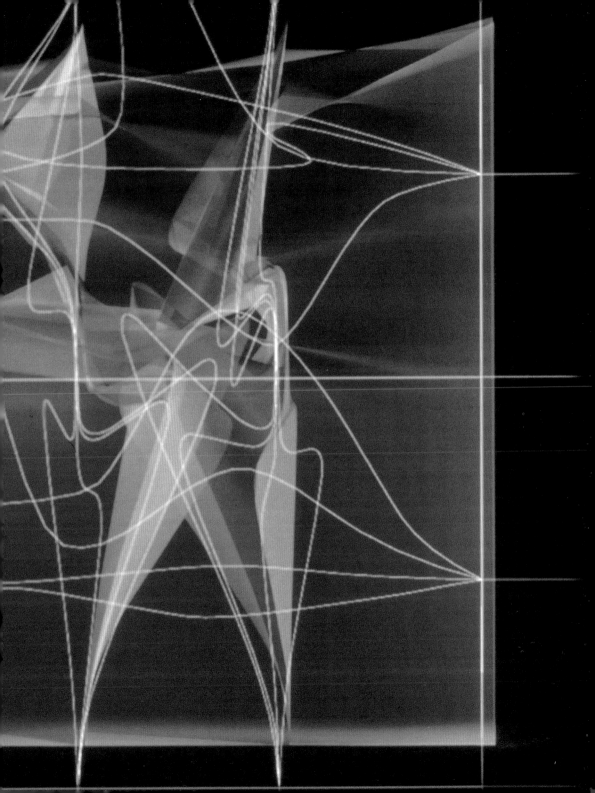

Memorial to the Murdered Jews of Europe

Berlin, Germany

1998-2005

Architecture is about monuments and graves, said the Viennese architect Adolf Loos at the turn of the 19th century. This meant that an individual human life could be commemorated by a stone, a slab, a cross, or a star. The simplicity of this idea ended with the Holocaust and Hiroshima and the mechanisms of mass death. Today an individual can no longer be certain to die an individual death, and architecture can no longer remember life as it once did. The markers that were formerly symbols of individual life and death must be changed, and this has a profound effect on the idea of both memory and the monument. The enormity and horror of the Holocaust are such that any attempt to represent it by traditional means is inevitably inadequate. The memory of the Holocaust can never be a nostalgia.

The enormity of the banal is the context of our monument. The project manifests the instability inherent in what seems to be a system, here a rational grid, and its potential for dissolution in time. It suggests that when a supposedly rational and ordered system grows too large and out of proportion to its intended purpose, it in fact loses touch with human reason. It then begins to reveal the innate disturbances and potential for chaos in all systems of seeming order, the idea that all closed systems of a closed order are bound to fail.

In searching for the instability inherent in an apparently stable system, the design begins from a rigid grid structure composed of some 2,700 concrete pillars, or stelae, each 95 centimeters wide and 2.375 meters long, with heights varying from zero to 4 meters. The pillars are spaced 95 centimeters apart to allow only for individual passage through the grid. Although the difference between the ground plane and the top plane of the pillars may appear to be random and arbitrary, a matter of pure expression, this is not the case. Each plane is determined by the intersections of the voids of the pillar grid and the gridlines of the larger site context of Berlin. In effect, a slippage in the grid structure occurs, causing indeterminate spaces to develop within the seemingly rigid order of the monument. These spaces condense, narrow, and deepen to provide a multilayered experience from any point. The agitation of the field shatters any notions of absolute axiality and reveals instead an omnidirectional reality. The illusion of the order and security in the internal grid and the frame of the street grid are thus destroyed.

Remaining intact, however, is the idea that the pillars extend between two undulating grids, forming the top plane at eye level. The way these two systems interact describes a zone of instability between them. These instabilities, or irregularities, are superimposed on both the topography of the site and on the top plane of the field of concrete pillars. A perceptual and conceptual divergence between the topography of the ground and the top plane of the stelae is thus created. This divergence denotes a difference in time, between what Henri Bergson called chronological, narrative time and time as duration. The monument's registration of this difference makes for a place of loss and contemplation, elements of memory.

The Ort is subdued in manner, effectively designed to minimize any disturbance to the Memorial's field of pillars. Its mass, weight, and density seem to perceptibly bear down and close in on individuals. The organization of its space extends the stelae of the field into the structure, provoking a continued state of reflection and contemplation once inside. The stelae are manifested in the form of a coffered roof deck with rib spacing which matches that of the field above. The presence of these elements is subverted by the Ort's walls, which are set on a classical nine-square grid. This grid is rotated against the logic of the field, thereby thwarting any paradigmatic understanding of its formal arrangement. The uncertain frame of reference that results further isolates individuals in what is intended to be an unsettling, personal experience. Juxtaposed against the hard, concrete materiality of the Ort will be a series of exhibitions that will use state-of-the-art technologies to create an ephemeral and visceral dimension appropriate for reflection. The glow of the illuminated images and text is intended to dematerialize the walls of the Ort, allowing the stelae to reveal themselves as a topographical extension of the field.

In a prescient moment in *In Search of Lost Time*, Marcel Proust identifies two different kinds of memory: a nostalgia located in the past, touched with a sentimentality that remembers things not as they were but as we want to remember them, and a living memory, which is active in the present and devoid of nostalgia for a remembered past. The Holocaust cannot be remembered in the first, nostalgic mode, as its horror forever ruptured the link between nostalgia and memory. Remembering the Holocaust can therefore only be a living condition in which the past remains active in the present. In this context, the monument attempts to present a new idea of memory as distinct

from nostalgia. We propose that the time of the monument, its duration, is different from the time of human experience and understanding. The traditional monument is understood by its symbolic imagery, by what it represents. It is not understood in time, but in an instant in space; it is seen and understood simultaneously. Even in traditional architectures such as labyrinths and mazes, there is a space-time continuum between experience and knowing; one has a goal to work one's way in or out.

In this monument there is no goal, no end, no working one's way in or out. The duration of an individual's experience of it grants no further understanding, since understanding is impossible. The time of the monument, its duration from top surface to ground, is disjoined from the time of experience. In this context, there is no nostalgia, no memory of the past, only the living memory of the individual experience. Here, we can only know the past through its manifestation in the present.

Sky above pillars

Plastic model
and conceptual model

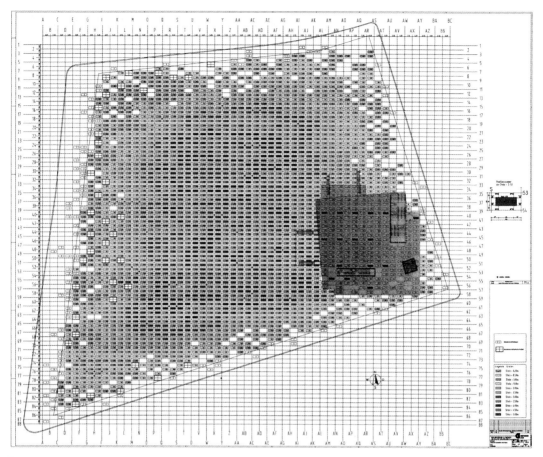

Plan

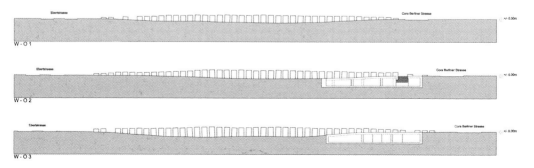

W - 01

W - 02

W - 03

Sections on the ground

156

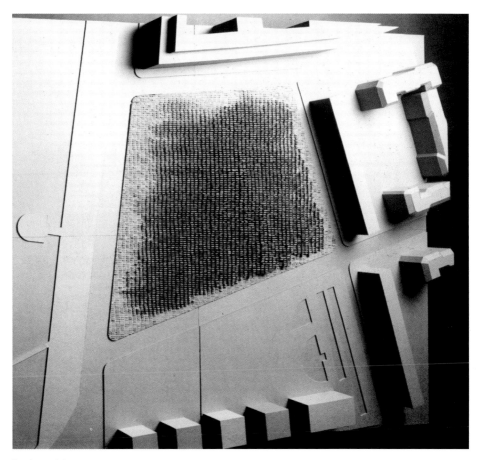

Study model

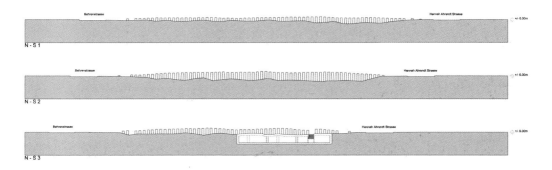

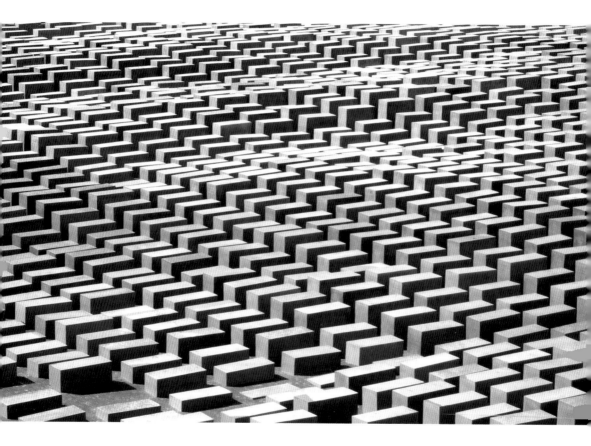

The City of Culture of Galicia
Santiago de Compostela, Spain
1999-ongoing

In a post-semiotic sensibility, where the culture of affect replaces the need for differentiation between sign and signified, the City of Culture in Santiago proposes the genetic coding process as a tactile response to the new logic. Three indexical diagrams of the medieval plan of the city center, the coquille shell and the pilgrimage route, constitute the original genetic sources for the project.

The deformation of the first diagrammatic layer (the city grid) by the superposition of the two latter ones, and the final torquing process induced by the introduction of deformation and flow lines, creates an internal genetic program which transforms them in encoding devices (removed from their former symbolic resonance).

"The original center of Santiago is medieval, yet it conforms to the Cartesian model that is the foundation of striated figure/ground urbanism, whereby buildings are figural and streets are residual. By placing the original town center into the ground of our site, this figure/ground urbanism is superseded. The trajectories of new pilgrimage routes then merge with the initial grid, deforming both the grid and the corresponding streets and buildings in the process. We treat these deformations as a series of surfacelike forms that, like the shell, are both smooth and striated.

Signifying the implosion of contemporary secular culture, and as a deliberate gesture against obsolete explosive models, the City of Culture develops a powerful new figure/figure urbanism. Rather than see the project as a series of discrete buildings—the traditional form of figure/ground urbanism—the buildings are literally incised into the ground to form a figure/figure urbanism in which architecture and topography merge to become figures. The secular center is physically and formally differentiated from the religious center, while it clearly expresses the trace of the old center as its genetic foundation.

The six buildings of the project are conceived as three pairs in order to convey a sense of smaller-scale, duo rhythms within the sextet: The Museum of Galician History and the New Technologies Center are one pair; the Music Theater and Central Services and Administration building are a second; and the Galician Library and Periodicals Archive are a third. Visitors' experiences of any given building will be affected, first and foremost, by its relationship to its immediate partner. As one moves through the site, the rhythms of the other pairs of buildings will further complicate and enrich one's experience."

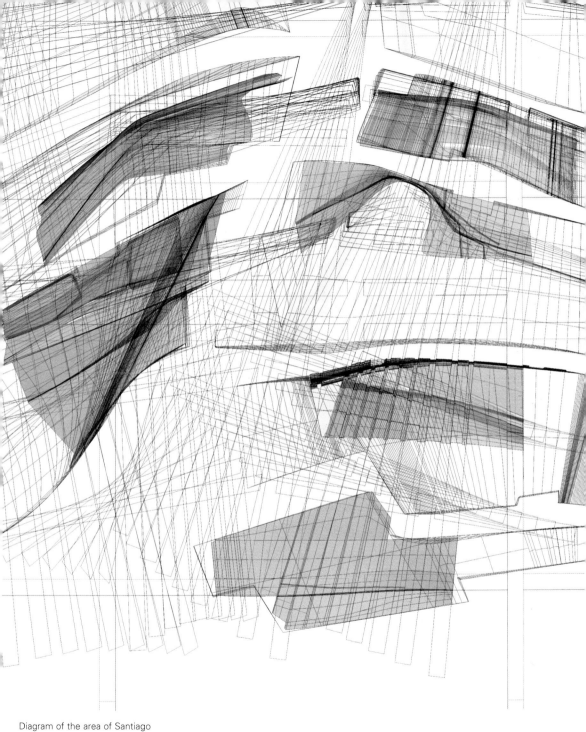

Diagram of the area of Santiago

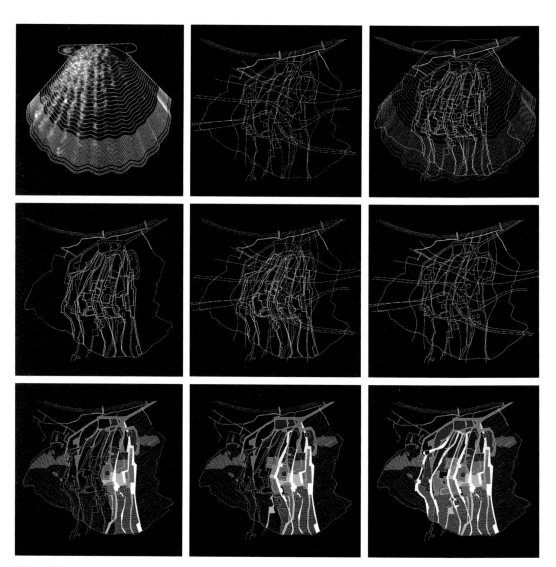

Series of diagrams
of the site

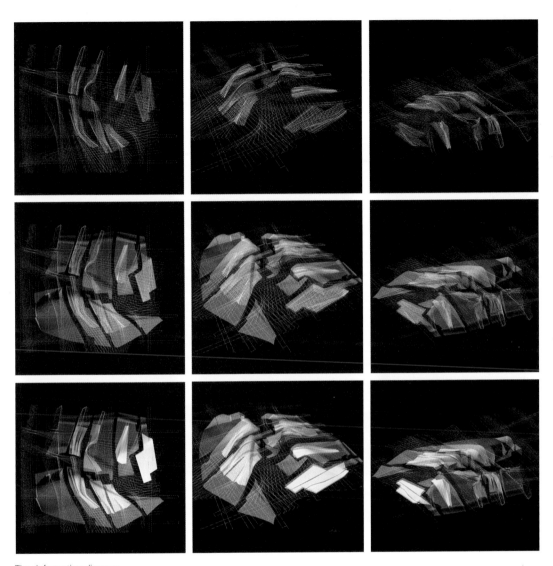

The deformation diagram
identifies the internal
volumes inside the buildings

Following double page
Volumetric analysis

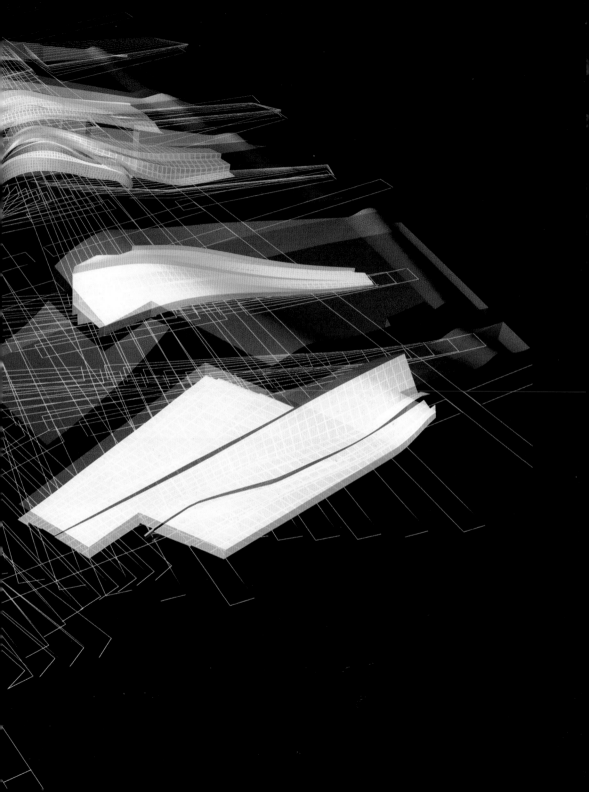

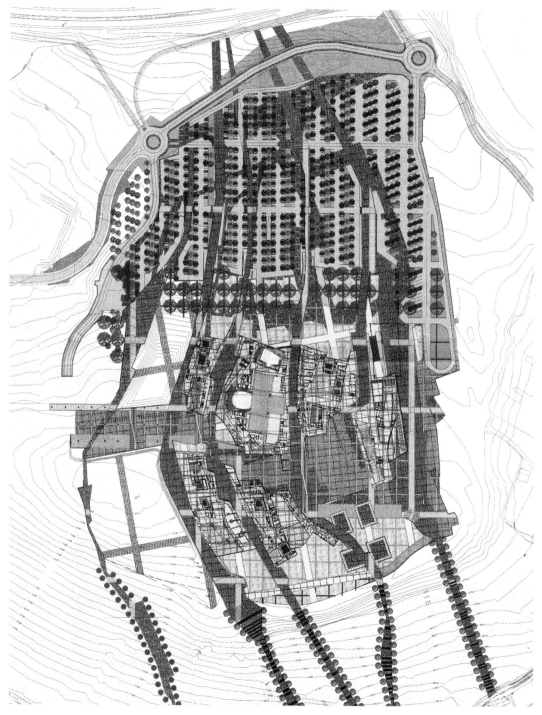

General plan

Computerised image
of the newspaper
and periodical library

Current state of the works

Following double page
Aerial view of the area
of intervention

Views of the roof of the
newspaper and periodical
library

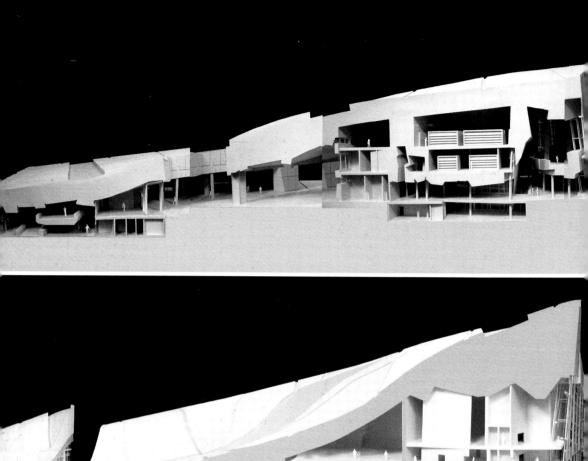

Section model 1:50
of the four buildings

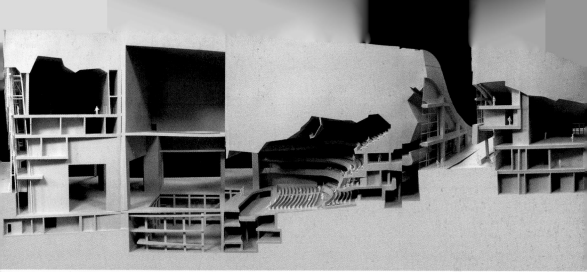

Sections of the building
of the Museum of Galician
History

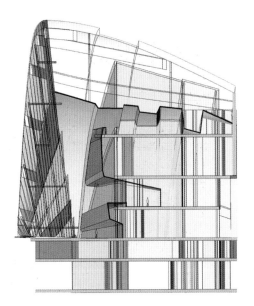
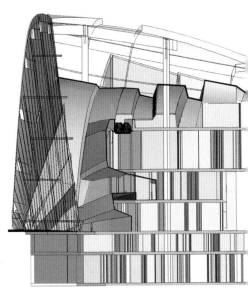
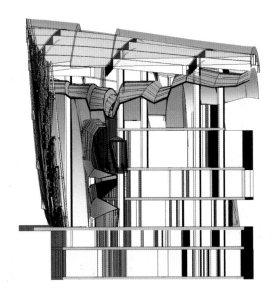

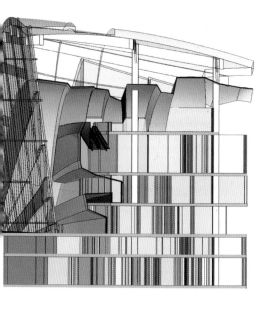

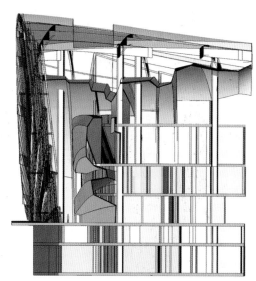

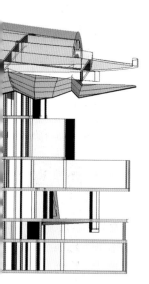

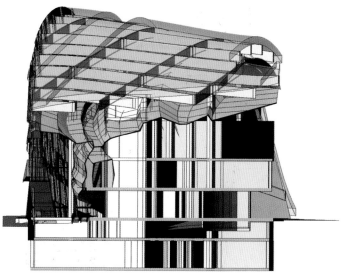

Guangdong Museum
Competition
Guangzhou, China
2004

The proposal for the Guangdong Museum is a "Box of Changes" that starts with the idea of the location as a manufactured object, the site, and as an idea, the *I Ching*.

The museum is part of a larger project that envisages a new opera house and a plaza for art and culture. The options were to create a competitive organic form or else a condition of "yin-yang", which was indeed chosen. The latter strategy develops an orthogonal half-cube capable of creating a dialectic with the fluid geometry of the opera house and the landscape.

The decision was influenced by another idea: that of animating the museum spaces according to the ancient Chinese logic of the *I Ching*, the *Book of Changes* and its grid pattern of hexagrams.

The classical key for identifying the hexagrams of the *I Ching* is a grid of 64 squares that form pairs between the upper and lower trigrams into hexagrams. A more recent interpretation of the hexagrams, known as the Eight Palaces, organizes the grid of 64 squares into eight hexagrams, each of which begins with a twin trigram. Mapping the logical sequence of the Eight Palaces on the classical grid, eight routes of circulation are articulated through the Museum.

The result is four real and four virtual routes that ascend and descend in the space. The real routes connect the four floors of the exhibition spaces and lead to a hanging garden, a park in the park. The virtual routes are not "navigable", but engraved on the floor as traces of paths that cannot be traveled. The four floors of the Museum are connected by ramps and the halls seem to float inside the cube. The cube, half glass wall and half solid, is a "yin-yang" box that contains other boxes.

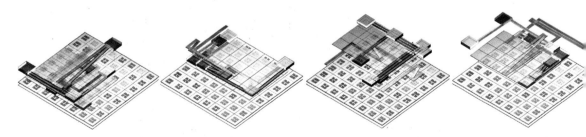

Axonometric schema

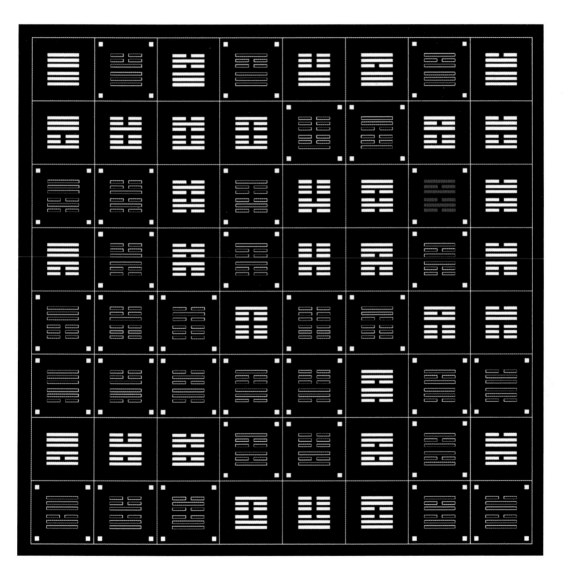

Diagrams of the transit routes

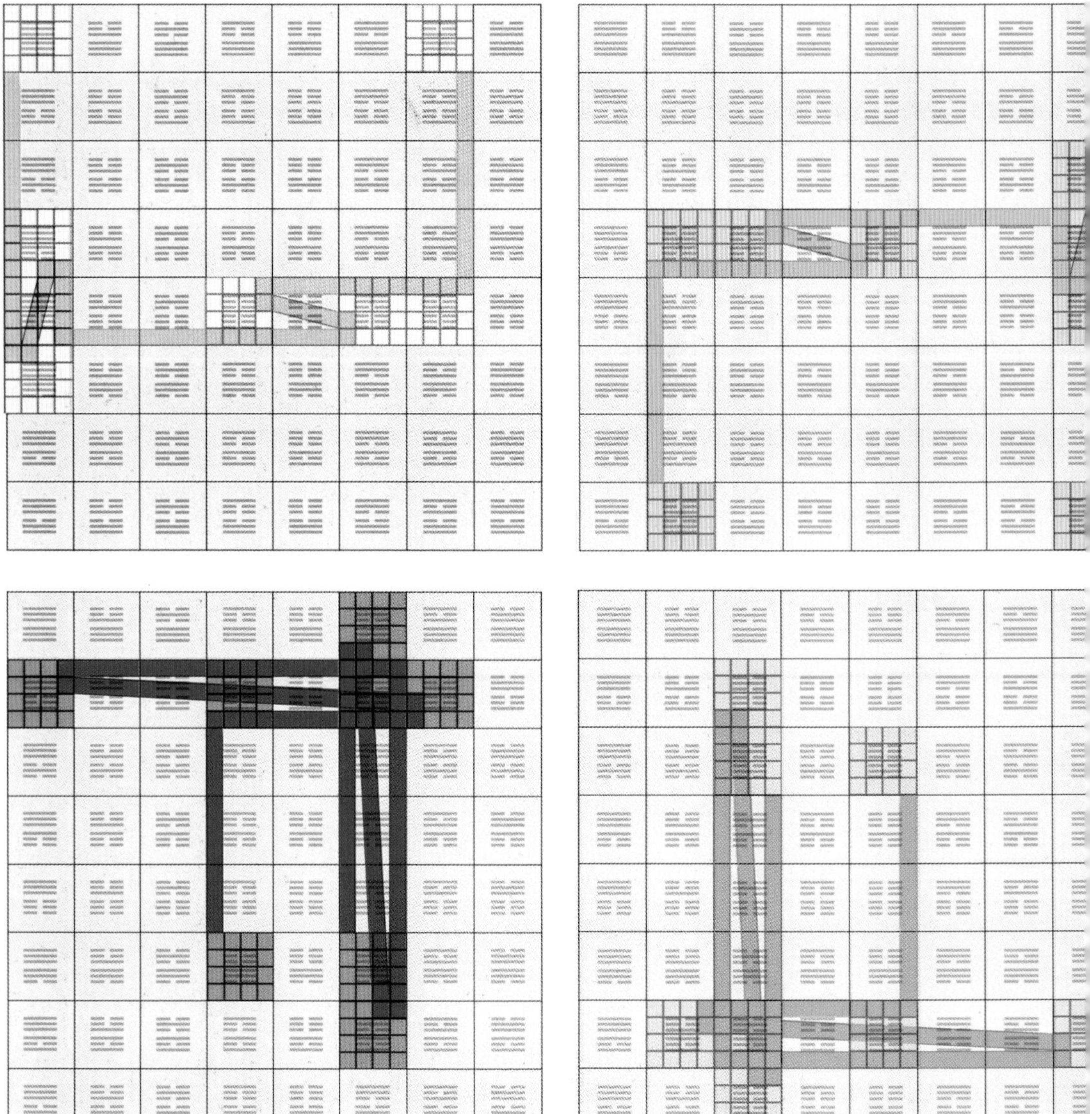

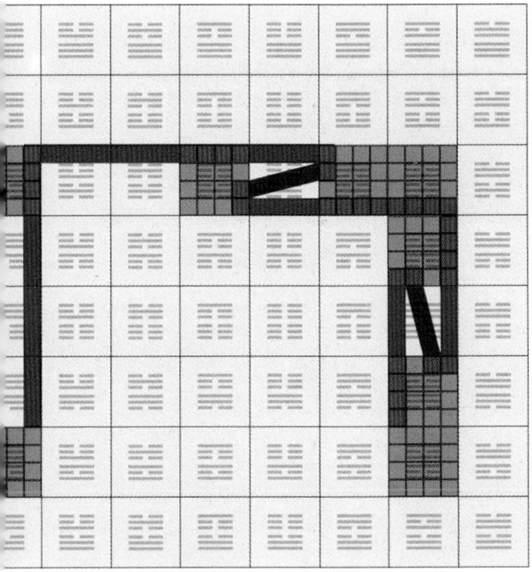

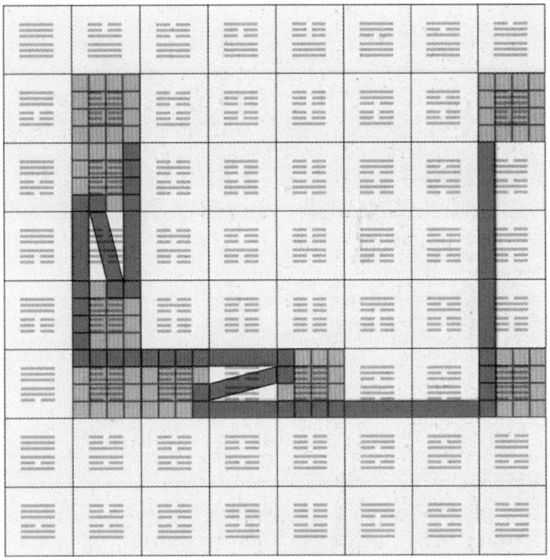

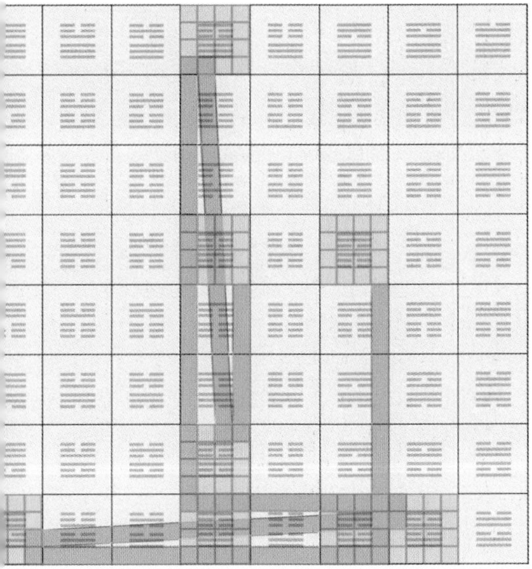

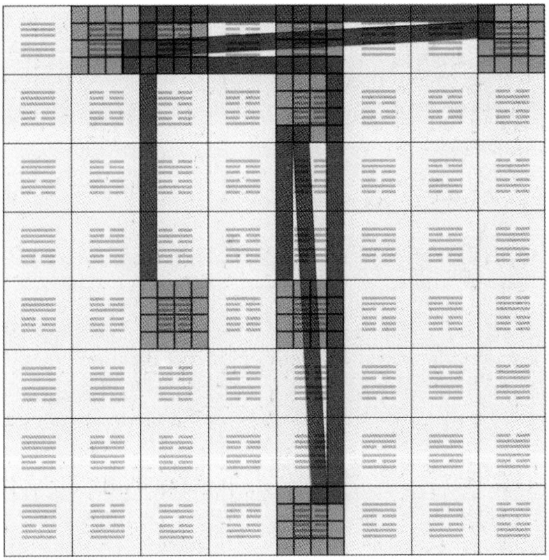

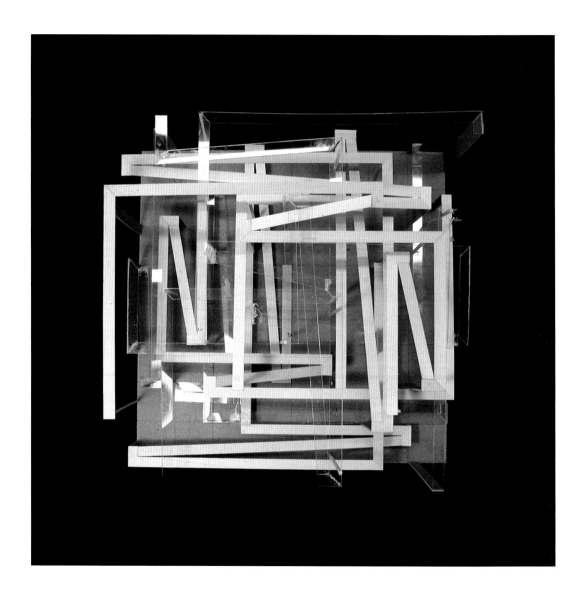

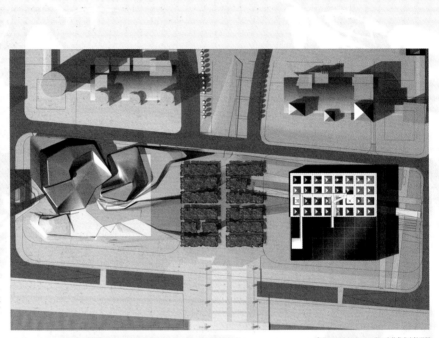

Culture and Art Square Plan 文化艺术广场平面

SCALE 1/1000

Plan at height -6.50

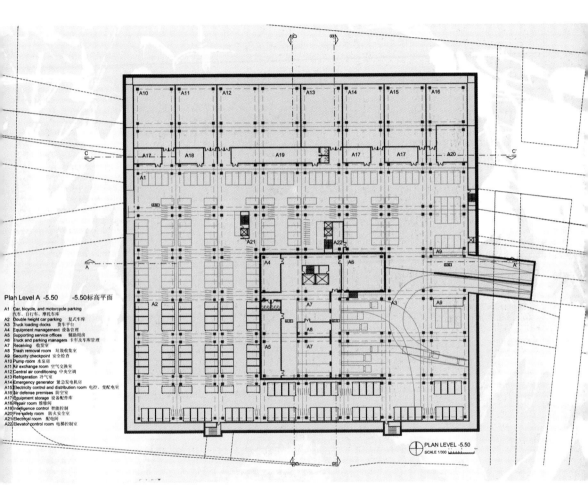

Plan Level A -5.50　　-5.50标高平面

A1 Car, bicycle, and motorcycle parking
汽车、自行车、摩托车库
A2 Double height car parking　复式车库
A3 Truck loading docks　货车平台
A4 Equipment management 设备管理
A5 Supporting service offices　辅助用房
A6 Truck and parking managers 卡车及车库管理
A7 Receiving　收发室
A8 Trash removal room　垃圾收集室
A9 Security checkpoint　安全检查
A10 Pump room 水泵房
A11 Air exchange room 空气交换室
A12 Central air conditioning 中央空调
A13 Refrigeration 冷气室
A14 Emergency generator 紧急发电机房
A15 Electricity control and distribution room 电控、变配电室
A16 Air defense premises 防空室
A17 Equipment storage 设备配件库
A19 Intelligence control 智能控制
A20 Fire safety room 防火安全室
A21 Electrical room 配电间
A22 Elevator control room 电梯控制室

PLAN LEVEL -5.50
SCALE 1/300

187

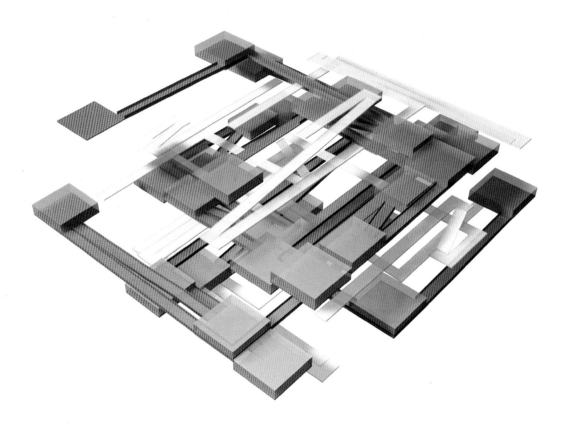

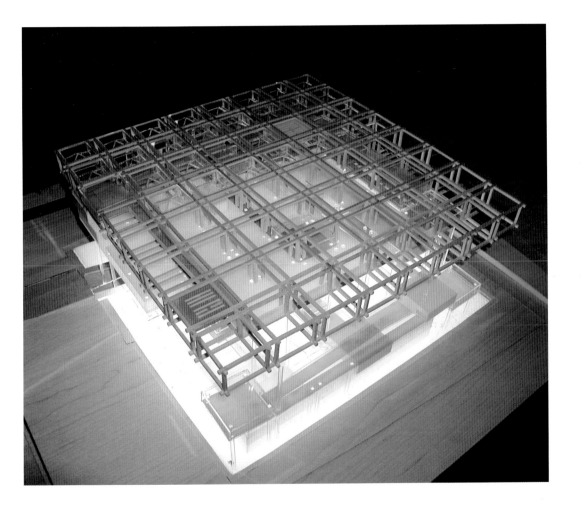

Perpective by night

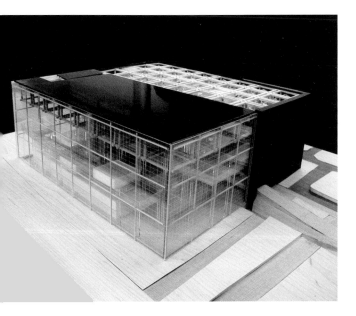

View of the plastic model

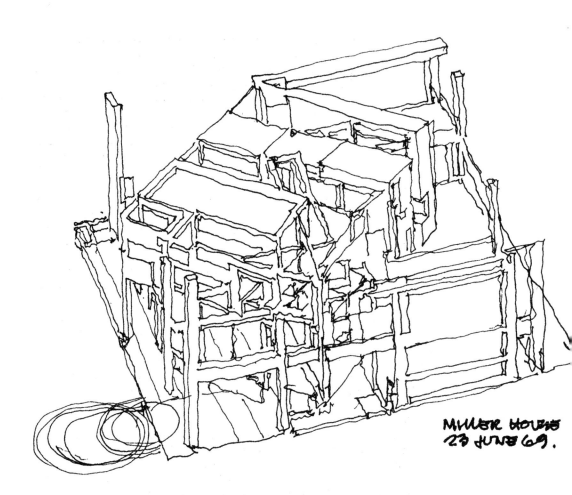

MILLER HOUSE
23 JUNE 69.

House III

Re-originating Diagrams
Jeffrey Kipnis

For the sake of argument, let us divide architects into two groups, the service professional and the speculative architect, knowing that at best these delimit a spectrum of tendencies, rather than categories. The service architect seeks to fulfill expertly the needs and desires of a client, while the speculative architect foregrounds his effort to change architecture so that it, in turn, can help shape a better world. Although there are many variations on the speculative theme, its basic terms, an historical perspective, a belief that architecture can be a directed instrument of change, and a conviction in the greater purpose of the work. Churchill said: "We shape our buildings; thereafter they shape us". Marx would have agreed, once he had reversed the order of causality,

Speculative architecture takes for granted many assumptions that underwrite its very possibility, assumptions that have been the object of intense debate for many decades. Perhaps the most passionately contested issue turns on the shaping function. Even if it is accepted that architecture causes change, does that fact necessarily enable the architect to act as an agent and influence the direction of change. The long debate has parallels in virtually every domain of cultural discourse. Schoenberg declared that with his atonal techniques, he and his followers "were writing the music of the future", to which Stravinsky quipped: "I would be content to write the music of the present". Tacit in the exchange is the agreement that, at least, neither continued to write the music of the past.

That brief meta-critical exchange not-withstanding, both composers soon returned to the problem that absorbed all of their attention and energies. Operating as experts within the intellectually and technically demanding regime of western art music composition, the two set about the task of deploying received techniques and developing new techniques to produce their compositions. Forty years after that initial exchange, Stravinsky began experimenting with Schoenberg's atonal techniques, though not because the predicted future, had arrived. Dodecaphonic music would never become the music of a future that had erased and replaced the music of the past. But it did produce effects mat have intrigued composers ever sense, and thus entered the repertoire of technique that established the evolving basis of that expert practice.

Let us restate the generic shaping function question in a more poignant form. Given that architecture is always political, can an architect posit; a political architecture? Can speculative architecture participate in the advent of democracy, can it resist the self-replicating ambitions of entrenched power and the banalizing forces of the market? For all of its optimism, confidence and claims, speculative architecture has at best produced mixed results with any efficacy that it can convincingly demonstrate. The democratic claims of Villa Savoye as an exemplar of the points, to rehearse a well-known example, are fatally discredited by the presence of servant's quarters and its retention of the traditional division between service and living spaces, or so it seems.

It is to this discussion that I think that a new reflection on the diagram, particularly as is it elaborated in the writings of Deleuze and reinforced by developments in the sciences and other arts, may make an important contribution to architecture, not so much by affording the architect new instrumental powers, but by portraying the very idea of efficacy in a new light.

Is it possible that speculative architecture produces something like a directed politics, but not as an instantiation of an ideal concept of the political, but as an original political effect specific to architecture, irreproducible by any other medium and irreducible to any other terms. The five-points collaborate at Savoye to erase the privileged status of me ground that architecture before it so strived to reinforce, transforming it into but one datum among many, including roof-top and floor plan. It works for me and on me, but I can understand why others just see a nice looking house. Does Beethoven's Ninth loose any of its democratic luster because it was debuted by an indentured orchestra and dedicated to the King of Prussia?

Perhaps not everyone, but only some people are sensitive to architectural effects in they full political dimension. I think a lot about certain practices, architecture constantly and above all, but also painting, physics, music and movies to a lesser extent and more or less in declining order of attention. I am indifferent to modern dance, utterly dumb to its wiles. On the other hand, I know many who follow it with interest and a few for whom there is nothing else that matters so much in the world. Are any of us more right about dance than the others? Or, is the segmentation of a larger collective into sub-audiences of varying interests and passions by material practices and the further segmentation by eventualities within those practices already best evidence of political effects. Indifferent to country music, I love Ligeti and hate Barry Manilow. Do not these passions affiliate me into ad hoc political parties with some and divide me from others?

Such questions belong to the problem of medium, specificity, and here is my conjecture.

The diagram and its processes are to re-origination what the sign and its processes are to representation. The diagram, therefore is the basis for all medium specificity. Medium specificity is the production by any medium of signals that are, in total, irreducible and irreproducible by any other medium. Reorigination is nothing other than the total effect of the signal.

D.H. Lawrence on Cézanne: "After a fight tooth-and-nail for forty years, he did succeed in knowing an apple, fully; and not quite as fully, a jug or two. That was all he achieved. It seems little, and he died embittered. But it is the first step that counts, and Cézanne's apple is a great deal, more than Plato's Idea..."

G. Deleuze on collage and Mozart: "When great musicians seize hold of a child's little ritonello [nursery rhyme], there are two ways in which they can seize it: either they make a collage of it, at such a moment in the development or unfolding of their work (hey fling you a little ritornello, as for example in Alban Berg's *Wozzeck*. In this case it's above all of the collage type, and the astonishing thing is that the work ends right there. It happens as well when a folkloric theme is tacked into a work, just as it happens that a becoming-animal is tacked into a work, as when Messiaen recorded birdsongs. Mozart's birds are not the same thing, it's not a collage; it happens that at the same time that the music becomes bird, the bird becomes something other than a bird. There is a bloc of becomings here, two dissymetrical becomings: the bird becomes something other than music, at the same time that the music becomes bird."

A fact (e.g., my middle name is Michael) is to those who read and understand it, a signal acting primarily as a sign. It enters the brain not by adding anything to it, certainly not an idea, but by reorganizing it. As it reorganizes the reader, though, the reorganization: will also cause some diagrammatic effects, however small, as the reorganization cascades through him. A pill, say a tab of Lsd, is a signal that acts primarily as a diagram, i.e., it contains no meaning or messages, but reorganizes the nervous system, producing meaning and messages and feelings as an after-effect.

For all of its considerable achievements, in its assault on the metaphysics of categorical boundaries, post-structuralist discourse, particularly that of Jacques Derrida, left disciplines and practices not, only with no autonomy, but with little sense of self intact. What could it mean to paint, to write poetry, to do architecture in the wake of Derrida's impeccable account of arche-writing? Derrida's writing forever dismantled the ontological question "What is... (art, e.g.)" and the institutional politics it sustained. Yet, it never actually posed the existential question, "Why do... (art)" and indeed went some distance to affirming the innate immunity of the question, albeit in revised terms (the "-con-" in deconstruction). Nevertheless, it must be said that a pandemic of shattered disciplinary-egos was one its side-effects.

History (at least in the form of academic historiography), the philosophy of essences and phenomenology are the traditional spokespersons for medium specificity, and these three institutions of thought bore the brunt of Derrida's forensic scrutiny. The challenge for discourse, therefore, assuming one is unwilling simply to reject or ignore Derrida's achievement, is to find a path to revisit the problem of disciplinary or medium specificity that avoids relapse.

Notwithstanding the power of the discourse ofarche-writing, even the practices of writing in the parochial sense remain after Derrida associated into genre and species—poetry, literature, philosophy, criticism. In fact, not only all practices, but all processes bifurcate into specific associations, along the lines of the major divisions of Linnaeus' binomial nomenclature. In that this organizational inclination spans 48 magnitudes of order, from galaxy clusters to sub-atomics, it seems that it is a fundamental aspect of the processes of matter itself.

Re-origination, the effect of a diagram, then is the basis for all specificities, including but not limited to; kingdoms of practice (e.g., science, art, mathematics) modes of practice (e.g. music, visual arts, literature, physics, chemistry, number theory, integral equations), medium specificity, (e.g., painting, sculpture, writing, quantum gravity, astronomy) genre within any particular medium (e.g, within writing: philosophy, poetry, literature, journalism; within music: art music, hard rock, folk, alternative, blues), and individual works. And all specificities are originations, that is, emitters of signals that cause unique diagrams.

I believe that Deleuze's discussion is helpful to the question in architecture only because architecture already possesses an ancient relationship to diagrams and instrumental drawing (one that rivals for important reasons the deep histories of diagrams in astronomy and mathematics). Diagrams underwrite all typological theories, as evidenced, for example, in the catalogues of Durand. Consider the much-vilified bubble diagram; the diagrammatic formalism initiated by Wölfflin and Wittkower, elaborated into a syntax the extended into context by Rowe and his followers and further by the symbolic and semantic considerations advocated by architects such a Rossi, Venturi and Hejduk.

Architecture's diagrammatic formalism soon fused with 20th century art's predisposition toward intellection, critique and process to produce dynamic formalism, with its easily recognizable litany of time-dependent formal relations, from rotation, translation, shift, sheer, to absence, collage and index, and the architectural diagram matured to its most fecund state as a generative tool for centrist, critical and speculative practices alike. Peter Eisenman's ouevre is nothing other than a sustained investigation of the possibilities of dynamic formalism, but if I cite his work, it is only to note one signpost in a development that suffuses me achievements of such diverse and original architects as Meier, Graves, Libeskind, Koolhaas, Holl and Hadid to name but a very few among many.

Because of its usefulness to process-based work, the diagrammatic aspect of dynamic formalism remains evident through a next generation of architects such as GLForm, FOA, R+U and UN Studio, even as their attention shifts away from cultural discourse and such issues as institutional critique and toward other more internal disciplinary considerations. Today, the legacy of the generative diagram continues to be evident in the work of new practices, though these proliferate and speciate along branches that distance them ever further from the initial discursive foundations of diagrammatic and dynamic formalisms.

A new consideration of the diagram as a both a topic for and an instrument of architecture then falls out of that domain not only as something new, powerful and useful, but also as something inevitable, like the Ptolemaic diagram of epicycles fell out of Aristotle's philosophy, Feynman diagrams fell out of QED, Venn diagrams fell out of set-theory, Reed-Kellogg diagrams fell out of grammar, or the Domino diagram fell out of modern architecture.

With but a moment's reflection, the profundity of the thought of the shaping function of the signal and its diagram effects deepens as its horizons begin to expand rapidly. Freud wondered at the mechanism by which the traits of parent, family and community were acquired by a child. He proposing that the process was the same as mourning; bit by bit, day by day, incrementally and catastrophically, we fend off the pain of loss by becoming what we loose.

Sociologists and linguists ponder the question in different terms, often starting with language. But setting aside the difficulty of accounting for the acquisition of grammar, vocabulary, diction, idiom and dialect, consider just the problem of regional accent, the sing-song of particular speech. What is a southern accent (and why does the notion of a "southern accent" work in so many different countries)? Where does it come from, where does it hide? In the buildings? In the landscape? How does it move from parent to child, from person to person, like an infection to which no speaker is immune? How does regional accent over time infect even fully-formed adult speakers that relocate from one region to another, always insidiously, beneath their awareness? How does accent know how 10 co-mingle with other previously existing accents; why does it infect some more virulently than others? If Woody Allen's *Zelig* did not answer such questions, it certainly posed them vividly.

Unless we brake in time, the dizzying gravity of such questions builds until it cannot be resisted. What begins as an intellectual attraction, soon grows into a maw, then a vortex, then a maelstrom, then a black hole that pulls every thing into it—all thought of mimesis, representation, meaning, semiotics, communication and information, obviously, but even more: thoughts of spirituality, of souls and their movements, the transmigration of souls, of God itself, its immanence, its becoming flesh, its breath of life, inspiration.

But at the bottom, the questions are these: what moves in a transmission from sender to receiver? What are the processes of sending and receiving? What is the *medium* of that movement? What link, if any, necessarily remains intact between the source of a transmission and its reception and what relationship does it construct between the transmitter and receiver? Whether your are a physicist, a theologist, a philosopher, a semiotician, avirologist, an artist, an architect, whatever your theoretical interests, these are your fundamental questions; and the place of the diagram.

Some helpful facts from contemporary science, and some speculation on signals, semiotics and diagrammatics.

All existence sends, receives and, upon both sending and receiving, reorganizes.

One of the most important developments in physics since the advent of quantum mechanics and relativity is the elevation of organization as an independent irreducible that participates in equivalences to the mass and energy. In the discourse of contemporary physics, organization is often called information. This terminology provokes a misunderstanding when it is equated with the common use of the term information to mean data or message. Information in this latter sense is only an after-effect of organization.

Because of the convertibility equivalences of mass, energy and organization. It would be better to say that Matter itself, a process, is signaling, receiving and re-organizing; never purely one or the other, always all three at once, and never reducible further.

All signals disperse broadly at a finite Speed and are corporeal, whether particle or field. Signaling and receiving always cause both sender and receiver to reorganize. Each and every signal is always received by more than one, and more often, very many receivers. The preponderance of all signals are received by more than one species of receiver and by many members of each species of receiver.

The only thing a signal does is to reorganize its receivers. Deleuze's abstract machine? The reorganization of a specific receiver by a specific signal obeys a regular, predictable, but, always probabilistic, set of rules, the basis for any species, animate or not, but also the basis for evolution. In response to the same signal, difference species of receivers will emphasize a different mix of the qualities of that signal, i.e., its mass, energy and organization.

An example: consider the call of a nesting female bird. The call is a signal, a sound ensemble that moves with a specific speed in a roughly spherical pattern of dispersion. It is specific in pitches, duration, pattern and intensity, i.e., it is organized. The call is typical of a species, but further individuated by the unique characteristics and circumstance of that individual bird.

To the bird's chicks, the signal signifies mother, to another member of its species, the call will feel erotic or madding; to a nearby hawk the same call will signify food and stimulate an urge to hunt, to a nearby vole it will cause panic, to a poet walking in the woods, a sensation that cascades into a lyrical turn of language. To a heavy snow bank, the signal may not induce much reorganization, but then it might induce an avalanche.

Signals do not contain either signs or diagrams. Signs and diagrams are after-effects of the reception of a signal, i.e., of the reorganization off the receiver by a signal. In any reception, signs and diagrams are always distinct, but a signal can never be partitioned into sign and diagram apriori, nor do signs and diagrams work autonomously on the receiver. "It is a very, very close and difficult thing to know why some paint comes across directly onto the nervous system, and other paint fells you the story in a long diatribe through the brain."

In September, 2002, the American composer John Adams debuted his *On the Transmigration of Souls*, commissioned by the New York Philharmonic to honor the victims of the attack on the World Trade Center, In the program notes, Adams spoke to the inspiration for the work. In one video of the event, he saw: "millions and millions of pieces of paper floating out of the windows of the burning skyscraper, cresting a virtual blizzard of white paper slowly drifting down to earth. The thought of so many lives lost in an instant—thousands—and also the thought of all these documents and memos and letters, faxes, spreadsheets and God knows what, all human record of one kind or another—all of this suggested a kind of density of texture that I wanted to capture in the music, but in an almost frieze-frame slow motion."

Imagining that the souls of those who died in the building might have passed into those airborne scraps of paper gave rise to the title, a reference to the widespread ancient belief in metempsychosis, the movement of souls from corporal being to corporal being.

"Transmigration means 'the movement from one place to another' or 'the transition from one state of being to another.' It could apply to populations of people, to migrations of species, to changes of chemical composition, or to the passage of material through a cell membrane. But in this case I mean it to imply the movement of the soul from one state to another. And I don't just mean the transition from living to dead, but also the change that takes place within the souls of those that stay behind, of those who suffer pain and loss and then themselves come away from an experience transformed. My desire in writing this piece is to achieve in musical terms the same sort of feeling one gets upon entering one of those old, majestic cathedrals in France or Italy. When you walk into the Chartres Cathedral, for example, you experience an immediate sense of something otherworldly. You feel you are in the presence of many souls, generations upon generations of them, and you sense their collected energy as if they were all congregated in that one spot. And even though you might be with a group of people, or the cathedral itself filled with other churchgoers or tourists, you feel very much alone with your thoughts and find them focused in a most extraordinary and spiritual way".

The composition combines classical instrumentation together with recorded and remixed voices and sounds...

"I eventually settled on a surprisingly small amount of text that falls into three categories. One consists of found sound clips of family members and friends reminiscing about lost loved ones at Ground-zero and elsewhere. Another is the simple reading of names, like a litany. I found friends and family members with different vocal timbres and asked each to read from the long list of victims. Then I made a mantra-like composition out of the tape-recorded reading of these names, starting with the voice of a nine year-old boy and ending with those of two middle aged women, both mothers themselves. I mixed these with taped sounds of the city—traffic, people walking, distant voices of laughter or shouting, trucks, cars, sirens, steel doors shutting, brakes squealing—all the familiar sounds of the big city that we usually never notice."

As I sat in the audience that night, I was unsure of what I was hearing, how to listen to the music or bow I felt about it, as is often the case at first encounters with speculations in any medium. Either the new shaping function of the music had not yet completed, its work on me, or it never would.

But I thought I grasped one aspect of the music, that moved me, but I cannot say whether emotionally or intellectually. Both. Neither. Maybe "moved" is the wrong word. As did everyone in the audience, I heard easily the taped voices and sounds, and then heard as the composer digitally looped and mixed these familiar sounds into denser and denser musical abstractions. Soon, the iconic elements of the recordings—the orated names, the sound bites, the identifiable city sounds, the humanity of the voices—dissipated as the remix exaggerated the musical dimension of those sounds, their pitches, tonalities and intrinsic rhythms, into the mantra he describes.

But I believe, I'm pretty sure at least, I heard something else: I heard the classical instruments of the orchestra—the strings, brass woodwinds and percussion instruments—which had until then accompanied with the tape it as an independent musical entity—begin to play the mix-music of the tape. I would not say the orchestra imitated the tape, but that the composer had scored the tape-mix for orchestra, like Beethoven scored natural sounds—birds and storms—into the music of the Sixth Symphony. It was the same, though it was different, and I felt that I sensed the composer's musical idea: the words and sounds of everyday life had transmigrated through the chaotic mixing of the tape into the instruments and then from them into me, and everyone. Everyone? I sat with someone very close to me that night, and remember looking at over at her to see if the music-souls had made their way into her as well. I could not tell, and never asked, but then, it had been a strange day.

"The diagram is indeed a chaos, a catastrophe, but is also a germ of order, of rhythm." "It is a very, very close and difficult thing to know why some paint comes across directly onto the nervous system, and other paint tells you the story in a long diatribe through the brain." "In the unity of the catastrophe and the diagram, man awakens to rhythm as matter and material." Who said these things? What do these mean?

After the intermission, the Philharmonic played Beethoven's Ninth. Of course, and thank God. Together, we in the audience moved as one through a transcendent world we knew and loved. But as we passed into the fourth movement, I realized that something entirely new was coming, a beloved musical event was about to be, had already been, transformed in the wake of the *Transmigration*. About half-way through the fourth movement, some nine minutes after the Beethoven has established the movement's main theme and the setting of the Schiller poem, the music comes to a dramatic pause on the word "God".

Following the infinite silence, the orchestra begins the long finale with a stark march, vaguely military some say. A naked oboe introduces the beat, offset by the syncopation of a marching drum, the main theme begins bluntly, played by a thin-scored woodwind band, with hand cymbals and triangle. To my car at least, it is unmistakably a musical painting of a peasant march. A solo tenor joins the march, and this imagistic setting of the main theme builds momentum. Quickly, evolves from the simple march into an intricate orchestral fugue that, with the intellectual permission of formal counterpoint, tears the theme and march rhythms to shreds, reorganizing them into something new, passionate, spiritual, sublime...

It is one my favorite passages in all of music, and one that I had long understood to be a musical rendition of the transformation of the prosaic into the profound. But that night I realized that in that very passage, Beethoven had attempted, with the intellectual, musical, poetic and political material of his time, what Adams was attempting in his: a transmigration of the soul, not just in the music, but by the music. A diagram had passed through the Ninth to the *Transmigration*. I will never again hear either piece without hearing at the same time, the other.

But did I really hear what I heard in the Adams? I knew already that experiments with representing the particular qualities of sampled and digital sounds and music in classical instrumental settings were well known. Ligeti, for example, makes a harpsichord sound like computer-generated music in his uncanny *Continuum for Cembalo (1968)*, the antique term cembalo used to emphasis the historical disjunction between the sound of the music and its instrumentation. But did Adams actually attempt to orchestrate the taped mantra as I imagined? When I listen again, I think I hear it, but am less sure. I promise myself that I will look into it further, check the score, but I guess I do not really want to know.

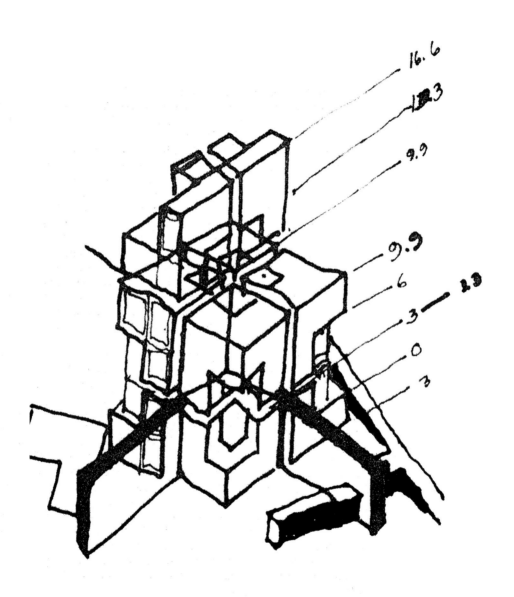

16.6

1₂3

9.9

9.9

6

3 — 2.0

0

3

Diagram of a football match

Feints: The Diagram
Peter Eisenman

Since Brunelleschi's import of perspective to architecture in the 15th century, architectural thought has been dominated by the split between reality, that is, real presence, and representation. This insertion of perspective into architectural discourse has had subtle but lasting effects. For one, it produced a conscious idea of a subject, albeit as a viewing subject in relation to an architectural object. Equally, through the agency of Renaissance painting and its deployment of perspectival architectural backgrounds, painterly conventions came into architecture. Things such as deep space, flat space, and the like produced the first immanent, as opposed to transcendental, metaphysic. In painting, the split between reality and representation, while present, was deemed to be less thematic because what was painted on a flat canvas was also its reality in presence. The introduction of visual conventions, this immanent metaphysic, has become so natural to architecture that Jacques Derrida said that architecture was the locus of the metaphysics of presence. The acceptance of this idea has rarely been questioned. But it is precisely the questioning of presence that has made Derrida's work important for architecture. Since the late 1970s, the question of the metaphysics of presence and the hegemony of the visual have been central to my work.

Jasper Johns, in an obituary on Marcel Duchamp in 1968, suggested that it was Duchamp who took art away from the retinal boundaries, which had been established with impressionism, and into a field where language, thought, and vision act upon one another. While the idea of the retinal deals with the direct impact of color, texture, and shape on the eye, the retinal is not a primary thematic for architecture. Rather, the optical is to architecture what the retinal is to painting. It is necessary for this discussion to distinguish between the optical, or retinal, and the visual. The optical is dependent on the primary conditions of the image, while the visual searches for other means of recording sensation with the eye other than the optical. The visual is different from the optical in that rather than deal only with surface phenomena, it can also deal with spatial and formal relationships, things which, while first seen, have to be conceptualized. The idea then would be to find a way in the visual to see presence as other than dominated by the optical. Abstraction was one attempt by modernism to undercut opticality by reducing figuration, but, with the social and political failures of modernism in the 1930s, abstraction also lost its power.

Thus, if the subject's relationship to presence is grounded in vision, then one challenge is not to exaggerate this condition via spectacular imagery but to redirect the optical into other aspects of the visual. Enter the diagram.

Currently there seems to be confusion over what a diagram is. This has been brought about as much by architects as it has by their theorists, who, influenced perhaps by Gilles Deleuze's reading of Francis Bacon's painting as diagrammatic or the idea of the diagram as an abstract machine as elaborated in Deleuze and Guattari's *A Thousand Plateaus*, have transferred these ideas to architecture with varying results. Yet another group of critics, perhaps hostile to the formal implications of Rudolf Wittkower's and Colin Rowe's invocations of the diagram and its formal implications have suggested that the diagram is neither a formal nor indexical instrument. It has been my contention that the diagram, while not necessarily iconic, has spatial and material consequences in architecture that are different from other disciplines. Among other things, the diagram attempts to displace presence as prima fascia opticality, that is, to displace the idea that what we see is truth, and thus to find a visual alternative to the optical. One of the motivations of the diagram is to provide an intermediary condition between presence, image, and idea; between the past and the present.

One challenge for architecture has always been to define its own internal discourse as different from other visual media, from painting, sculpture, film, etc. This has become even more critical today, with the saturation of print and visual media dedicated to the 30-second sound-cum-visual byte. Architecture, in an attempt to compete with this proliferation, has become more easy, more shaped, and spectacular. Clearly, if one cannot compete on media's ground, the challenge is not to return to the static, classical imagery of architecture's past but rather to find another way to deal with the problem of presence, of the need to be somewhere, a being there, which is neither grounded in phenomenology nor in Heideggerian being in time.

A diagram derives from the context of a site, program, or history. A diagram does not necessarily exist a priori in any project. In this sense, it is not like a type which has a fixed relationship to form, function, and history. There are two kinds of work on diagrams. One is theoretical and analytic, the other is operational and synthetic. The former takes existing building and analyzes them to find diagrams that animate these buildings. The latter is something teased out of a program or site that permits these conditions to be seen in a different way. The diagram is both a form of text, a tissue of traces, and an index of time. A diagram is to architecture as a text is to a narrative. The diagram is formed but it may not be formal.

My reading of Le Corbusier's *Domino* diagram opened up what seemed to be an early manifestation of the five points of architecture as something beyond the usual reading of its tectonic implications. Equally, my analysis opened the diagram to its own internal formal characteristics, which, while they may not have been thematic for Le Corbusier at the time, nevertheless influenced any reading of it.

While Charles Sanders Peirce thought that the diagram should have a visual similitude to its object, and therefore iconic in its being, in many ways the diagram, if it is to be an intermediary in the optical, must forgo a visual thematic. While a diagram will always have some visual reference to its object, the fact that this visual reference is not thematic is what is at issue in the diagram.

In my work, the diagram has been a template for invention. It is neither a type form, nine squares, or a formal similitude, that is, the diagram as the object itself. This exhibition demonstrates the evolution of the diagram in both my analytic and projected work. This work began with my Ph.D. thesis in 1963, "The Formal Basis of Modern Architecture", and continued with my study on two of Terragni's buildings, the Casa del Fascio and the Casa Giuliani Frigerio. My project work paralleled this research. Diagrams were the basis for the process of the early houses, and as the work increased in scale and complexity, so did the diagrams.

A diagram is not a plan. For example, both Piranesi's Campo Marzio and his Collegio Romano appear to be plans, but in my analysis, they are perhaps more importantly diagrams. In the case of the Collegio, one must ask how it is possible for something to appear to be axial and symmetrical in a classical sense and yet have no possible function in that regard. Equally, the Campo Marzio is a tissue of impossibility with no single time but multiple times and scales as the basis for the work. Other such analyses have opened up other architects, from Palladio to Moretti, to show the diagrammatic possibilities for reading other architects whose work has traditionally been assumed to be based on the optical.

Selected Built Projects

House VI
Started: 1972
Completed: 1975
Location: Cornwall,
Connecticut
Client: Mr. and Mrs.
Richard Frank

IBA Social Housing
Started: 1981
Completed: 1985
Location: Berlin, West
Germany
Client: Hauert Noack,
GMBH & Company

Wexner Center for the
Visual Arts and Fine Arts
Library
Started: 1983
Completed: 1989
Location: Columbus, Ohio
Client: The Ohio State
University

Aronoff Center for Design
and Art
Started: 1988
Completed: 1996
Location: Cincinnati, Ohio
Client: University
of Cincinnati

Koizumi Sangyo
Corporation Headquarters
Building
Started: 1988
Completed: 1990
Location: Tokyo, Japan
Client: Koizumi Sangyo
Corporation

Greater Columbus
Convention Center
Started: 1990
Completed: 1993
Location: Columbus, Ohio
Client: Greater Columbus
Convention Center
Authority

TSA/Cardinals Multipurpose
Stadium
Started: 1997

Status: In progress
Location: Glendale, Arizona
Client: Tsa/Arizona
Cardinals

City of Culture of Galicia
Started: 1999
Status: In progress
Location: Santiago
de Compostela, Spain
Client: Xunta de Galicia

Cannaregio Town Square
Concorso per l'area
di Cannaregio
Venice, Italy, 1978
Architect: Peter Eisenman
Project Team: David Buege,
John Nambu, Joan Ockman
Models: Sam Anderson,
Andrew Bartle
Model Photos: Dick Frank

Memorial to the Murdered
Jews of Europe
Client: Stiftung Denkmal
für die Ermordeten Juden
Europas
Chief executive:
Hans-Erhard Haverkamp,
Günter Schlusche
Design architect:
Eisenman Architects
Design Principal:
Peter Eisenman
Associate: Richard Rosson
Project Designers:
Sebastian Mittendorfer,
Ingeborg Rocker
Design Team: Matteo
Cainer, Gordana
Jakimovska, Yangsong Ma,
Matias Musacchio,
Emmanuel Petit,
Kai Peterson, Wiebke
Schneider, Oliver Zorn
Project Assistants:
Emily Abruzzo, Jean-Paul
Amato, Lars Bachmann,
Markos Beuerlein, Walter
Wulf Boettger, Volker
Bollig, Anja Brueggemann,
Artur Carulla, Stefano
Colombo, Nina Delius,

Constantin Doehler, Hayley
Eber, Alexa Eissfeldt,
Karsten Fiebiger, Juliane
Fisher, Christian Guttack,
Bart Hollanders, Nadine
Homann, Peter Hufe, Julia
Hochgesand, Ilman Kriesel,
Christian Lange, Jakob
Ohm Laursen, Dirk LeBlanc
Philipp Muessigmann,
Claire Sà, Nicole Schindler,
Stephanie Streich, Minako
Tanaka, Wolf von Trotha,
Karen Weber
Construction Manager:
Architekt Manfred Schasler,
Manfred Schasler, Axel
Heintz
Engineer: Happold
Ingenierbuero GmbH,
Paul Rogers, Martin
Strewinski, Ewan McLeod,
Steffen Philipp
Landscape: Olin
Partnership, Laurie Olin,
David Rubin
Partner: Happold
Ingenieurbüro GmbH
Engineers:
Paul Rogers
Martin Strewinski
Steffen Philipp
Planning software:
Microsoft Office, AutoCad,
Strap, Linear
Construction period:
1997 competition
1998-2003 design
2003-2005 construction
10 May 2005 opening
and dedication
Location: Berlin, Germany
Area:
Stelenfeld: 19,074 square
meters
Ort der Information:
Bruttogrundfläche
(Baufläche)
Gross area/excavated area:
2116.136 square meters
Nutzfläche (Net area)
1053.21 square meters
Verkehrsfläche (Circulation
area) 286.18 square meters

Client Contact:
Dr. Hans-Erhard
Haverkampf
Stiftung
Denkmal für die ermordeten
Juden Europas
Planning software:
AutoCAD
Rhino
3D studiomax

Essential Bibliography

P. Eisenman et al., *Houses of Cards*, Oxford University Press, New York, 1987.
Eisenman Architects and Richard Trott and Partners, *The Wexner Center for the Visual Arts: Ohio State University*, Rizzoli, New York, 1989.
Cities of Artificial Excavation: The Work of Peter Eisenman, 1978–1988, J.-F. Bedard (ed.), Rizzoli, New York, 1994 (catalogue for the exhibition at the Centre Canadien d'Architecture, Montreal, May 2 – June 19, 1994).
M Emory Games: Emory Center for the Arts. Eisenman Architects, Harvard Graduate School of Design and Rizzoli, New York, 1995.
Eleven Authors in Search of a Building: The Aronoff Center for Design and Art at the University of Cincinnati, C. Davidson (ed.), Monacelli Press, New York, 1996.
P. Eisenman, *Diagram Diaries*, Universe, New York ,1999.
P. Eisenman et al., *Blurred Zones: Investigations of the Interstitial, Eisenman Architects 1988–1998*, Monacelli Press, New York, 2003.
P. Eisenman, *Giuseppe Terragni: Transformations, Decompositions, Critiques*, Monacelli Press, 2003.
Eisenman Inside Out: Collected Essays of Peter Eisenman, 1963–1988, M. Rakatansky (ed.), Yale University Press, New Haven–London, 2004.
Peter Eisenman: Barefoot on White-hot Walls, P. Noever (ed.), Hatje Cantz Verlag, Ostfildern-Ruit, 2005 (catalogue for the exhibition at the MAK, Vienna, December 15, 2004 – May 22, 2005).
CodeX: The City of Culture of Galicia, C. Davidson (ed.), Monacelli Press, New York, 2005.
Holocaust Memorial Berlin, Lars Müller Publishers, Baden, 2005.

Biography of Peter Eisenman

Peter Eisenman is an architect of international renown and runs the Eisenman Architects studio in New York. Born in New Jersey in 1932, he visited Italy for the first time in the summer of 1961, while he was teaching architecture at Cambridge University in England. On that occasion, together with Colin Rowe, he visited the works of Palladio, Scamozzi, Vignola, Giulio Romano and Terragni, architects that have influenced his career. His interest in Terragni, which emerged in the analysis of the Casa del Fascio and the Casa Giuliani Frigerio in Como, resulted, forty years later, in the book *Giuseppe Terragni: Transformations, Decompositions, Critiques* (published in Italy as *Transformazioni, Decomposizioni, Critiche*, Quodlibet Editore, 2004). "Contropiede" [Counterattack] is his second solo exhibition in Italy after the installation "Il Giardino dei passi perduti" [The Garden of the Lost Footsteps] at Castelvecchio, Verona (June 2004–March 2005). In 1973 he was present at the "Rational Architecture" exhibition directed by Aldo Rossi at the XV Triennial in Milan and in 1976 in "Europe-America", the first Biennial of Architecture in Venice, where he returned in 1978 for "Dieci progetti per Venezia" [Ten Projects for Venice] with the project for the Cannaregio area. At the Third Biennial of Architecture, in 1985,

he won the Leone di Pietra for his "Moving Arrows, Eros and other Errors; Romeo+Juliet", a project involving the Castello dei Monataguti e Capuleti in Verona. In 1991 the project for the Aronoff Center for Design and Art was one of the two projects selected at the United States Pavilion at the Biennial, and in 2002 his "City of Culture", currently under construction, was selected at the eighth Biennial. In 2004 he received the Leone d'Oro for his lifelong commitment to the advancement of architecture at the IX Biennial of Architecture in Venice. Currently, Eisenman Architects is involved in the construction of a multi-purpose stadium in Phoenix and a 750,000 sq. ft. cultural complex, the City of Culture of Galizia in Santiago de Compostela, Spain. Eisenman Architects has been selected, together with a group of three other studios, to participate in the preparation of a proposal for the World Trade Center area. The Memorial to the Jewish victims of the Holocaust in Europe was consecrated on 10 May 2005.

Peter Eisenman's activities have always included teaching and writing. In 1976 he founded the Institute for Architecture and Urban Studies (IAUS), a think tank reserved for architecture, which he directed until 1982. He has been editor-in-chief of the institute's journal,

"Oppositions" and "Oppositions Books", which has published, among other things, "The Architecture of the City" by Aldo Rossi, the U.S. edition of which was completed together. The book "Five Architects", published in 1972, provided the premise for an exhibition on the work of the "Five" at the Institute of Architectural Analysis of Naples in 1976, the catalogue of which, "Five Architects, NY", included the article by Manfredo Tafuri, "Les Bijoux indiscrets" (Officina Edizioni, Rome). Peter Eisenman's academic activities include teaching at Princeton, Cambridge and the IAUV in Venice and the ETH in Zurich. At Harvard he was "Arthur Rotch Professor" from 1982 to 1985 and "Eliot Noyes Visiting Design Critic" in 1993. He has also been the first "Distinguished Professor of Architecture" at the Cooper Union in New York, and is currently Luis Khan Professor at Yale. Among his many books: "House X" (Rizzoli, 1982), "Fin d'Ou T HouS" (The Architectural Association, 1985), "Moving Arrows, Eros and Other Errors" (The Architectural Association, 1986), "Chora L Works" (Monacelli Press, 1997) with Jacques Derrida, and "Diagram Diaries" (Universe, 1999). The monographs on the studio include: "Peter Eisenman, Opere e progetti" by Pippo Ciorra (Electa, 1993) and "Mistico Nulla' L'Opera di Peter Eisenman" by Renato Rizzi (Motta Architettura, 1996).

Peter Eisenman also has a degree in Architecture from Cornell University, a Master's from Columbia University and an M.A. and a Ph.D. from Cambridge University. He has two doctorates in Fine Arts from Illinois University, Chicago and the Pratt Institute in New York. In 2003 he received an Honorary Degree from the La Sapienza University in Rome, conferred on him in March of last year.